Doctoral Supervision
Organization and Dialogue

Doctoral Supervision
Organization and Dialogue

Søren Smedegaard Bengtsen

Aarhus University Press |

Doctoral Supervision
Organization and Dialogue
© The author and Aarhus University Press 2016
Layout and typesetting by Narayana Press
Cover design by Jørgen Sparre, www.sparregrafisk.dk
Printed by Narayana Press, www.narayana.com

ISBN 978-87-7124-237-9

AARHUS UNIVERSITY PRESS
Langelandsgade 177
DK-8200 Aarhus N
www.unipress.dk

INTERNATIONAL DISTRIBUTION
UK & Eire
Gazelle Book Services Ltd.
White Cross Mills, Hightown
Lancaster LA1 4XS, England
www.gazellebooks.com

North America
ISD
70 Enterprise Drive
Bristol, CT 06010
USA
www.isdistribution.com

PEER REVIEWED

/ In accordance with requirements of the Danish Ministry of Higher Education and Science, the certification means that a ph.d.-level peer has made a written assessment which justifies this book's scientific quality.

CONTENTS

PART 1
INTRODUCING DOCTORAL SUPERVISION AS AN ADVANCED PEDAGOGY
1.0 Why this book? Why now? 9

PART 2
SUPERVISION AS ORGANIZATION
2.0 Formal organization 33
2.1 Enculturation – informal organization 46
2.3 Thesis organization 72
2.4 Roles and relations as organizers 79
2.5 Conclusion 84

PART 3
SUPERVISION AS DIALOGUE
3.0 Teaching format 89
3.1 Intrinsic value 101
3.2 Listening and voicing 111
3.4 Concluding remarks 123

PART 4
ADVANCED PEDAGOGY
4.0 Ambivalent pedagogy 129
4.1 Subtle pedagogy 140
4.2 Strange pedagogy 150
4.3 Embedded pedagogy 160
4.4 Torn pedagogy: Net-based doctoral supervision 170
4.5 Conclusion 180

PART 5
CODA: FUTURE APPROACHES TO DOCTORAL SUPERVISION
5.0 Strong thinking 185
5.1 Terminology 187
5.3 Advanced pedagogy 189

References 191

PART 1

INTRODUCING DOCTORAL SUPERVISION AS AN ADVANCED PEDAGOGY

1.0 WHY THIS BOOK? WHY NOW?

Research into doctoral supervision has been on the agenda for quite a long time now, measured according to the rapid, far-reaching and comprehensive organizational changes at universities worldwide over the last generation. For at least 30 years now doctoral supervision has been the subject of growing attention, and has become firmly established as a field of research in itself with its own international journals, conferences, societies, networks and communities. Though research into doctoral supervision emerged during the 1970s, the 1980s can be said to be the decade in which the foundations for the field were laid. As Taylor and Beasley (2010) recall, in the 1980s there were heated debates about doctoral education and supervision due to global investigations that "revealed that substantial numbers of candidates never completed their doctoral studies while those who did were taking up to twice as long as they should have done" (Taylor & Beasley 2010: 1). Naturally, the spotlight was turned on doctoral supervisors and their ability to support and guide students towards completion. The 1980s also gave occasion to a heightened focus on "non-traditional research students", as pointed out in Phillips and Pugh (2012: 127ff.), a book that was first published in 1987. More female students, students working full-time on the side and international students became part of the doctoral system, challenging organizational structures and demanding more diverse and inclusive forms of pedagogy in doctoral education programs and supervision processes.

During the 1990s research into doctoral supervision and doctoral education manifested itself firmly as a field in its own right, and numerous forms of quantitative and qualitative studies secured diversity in topics in and approaches to the field (Bengtsen 2014; Bengtsen 2012). As Hockey (1996) stated midway through the 90s, the range of singular studies was growing rapidly; it has continued to grow, with the first decade of the new millennium spawning a significant number of handbooks for both doctoral supervisors and students. As I write elsewhere, "this handbook literature can be understood in Anne Lee's sense as providing "companion" guides, "a series of guides to effective supervision" (Lee 2012: 30). Lee's use of the term 'handbook' mirrors Gina Wisker's phrase "self-help books" (Wisker 2012: 58), with which she refers to this corpus of literature, including her own work. These terms are not meant derogatively but rather as an acknowledgement of how far research into doctoral supervision has come since its emergence as a field in the 1980s. Besides their function as pedagogical and didactical guidebooks, these texts can be seen as a series of reviews of recent and major studies on the different aspects of the supervisory context. Furthermore, and unlike many singular studies, the handbook literature foregrounds the didactical element of doctoral supervision, explicating the teaching and learning potentials inherent in the phenomenon." (Bengtsen 2014a: 4). Some of these handbooks – such as Delamont, Atkinson & Parry (2004); Dysthe & Samara (2006); Handal & Lauvås (2011); Eley & Murray (2009); Lee (2012); Peelo (2011); Taylor & Beasley (2010); and Wisker (2012) – have enjoyed widespread recognition for uniting a research perspective with pedagogical and didactical guidelines and strategies for supervisors to apply in their daily work at the university.

Thematically, research into doctoral supervision has sprawled in many different directions from the mid 1990s onwards, encompassing such diverse approaches as: (1) doctoral education, and not 'only' supervision as such, as a research focus in itself (Lee & Danby 2012; Boud & Lee 2009; McAlpine & Åkerlind 2010; Golde & Walker 2006; Walker et al 2008); (2) social and power relations in the supervisory dyad (Armitage 2008, Grant 2008; Grant 1999); (3) gender and cultural issues connected to doctoral supervision (Leonard 2001; Grant 2003; Bartlett & Mercer 2001); (4) institutional and organizational settings and their implications for doctoral education and supervision (McAlpine & McKinnon 2013; McAlpine & Norton 2006; Delamont, Atkinson & Parry 2000; Green & Powell 2005; Rowley & Sherman 2004); (5) the importance of the personal dimension for understanding the field of research supervised (Bengtsen 2011; Manathunga 2005; Määttä 2012; (6) handbooks on doctoral supervision for supervisors (see the works mentioned above); (7) handbooks for doctoral students on how to get a PhD and how to cope with being a doctoral student (Petre & Rugg 2011; Wisker 2008; Cryer 2006; Cottrell 2014; Philips & Pugh 2012); and (8) a new wave of practice-based, experimental narratives told by supervisors and students in their own words, from their own worlds (Engels-Schwarzpaul & Peters 2013; Määttä 2012; Bartlett & Mercer 2001; Eley & Jennings 2005; Epstein, Boden & Kenway 2005).

Due to the many and varied aspects of research into doctoral supervision, it can certainly be said, as McAlpine and McKinnon (2013) argue, that doctoral supervision is "the most variable of all variables" (McAlpine & McKinnon 2013: 267 – a phrase first used by Bowen & Rudenstine 1992: 260) – meaning that the only thing stable about supervision processes is their constantly transforming and contextual character. All the different contextual features described above can be said to cover equally real and important pedagogical and organizational dimensions of doctoral supervision practice, and as McAlpine and Norton (2006) point out these different contexts can be said to be placed "within multiple nested contexts whereby the factors influencing attrition and retention are influenced by different stakeholders" (McAlpine & Norton 2006: 5). Instead of isolating different institutional and educational contexts, McAlpine and Norton argue that they are intertwined and operate within each other, nested within each other's organizational domain. In many ways I find the sprawling and entangled character of doctoral supervision highly inspirational; the fact that the research somewhat matches this complex and dynamical character of doctoral supervision pedagogy makes the field robust, inviting and relevant to diverse university practices around the globe.

However, this almost entropic diversity of research perspectives means that it is necessary sometimes to focus on the summit reached, and, if only for a brief while, to take in the view and remember the essence of the phenomenon we are trying so hard to grasp in its complexity, and then to look soberly ahead. Firstly, this book is not intended as yet another review of the research of the past two or three decades, since other books and papers have done that most effectively. Neither is the intention to write another handbook for the assumed supervisors in despair, containing all sorts of counsel regarding pedagogical and practical matters. We already have many such books – more than any supervisor can hope to read. Furthermore, as the last seven years of observing supervisors on master's and doctoral programs at the university have shown me, supervisors neither need help nor think they need it, though many people, especially in developmental departments, think they do. What supervisors actually need is not a book that tells them how they should supervise – they are perfectly capable of that themselves – but instead one that gives them ways to view and reflect on their own personal strategies and the implications these have for what they really want to do. In that respect this book serves as tool and catalyst for reflection, rather than providing normative ideals for best practice.

Secondly, I have striven to cut through the complexity of the perspectives unearthed in research into doctoral supervision today and to strike to the core of the matter. This does not mean that I call for a return to simpler times, or that I brandish a sort of stereotypical pedagogical essentialism. On the contrary, I find the diversity in the field potent and creative. More to the point, I wish to construe a meta-perspective for the understanding of doctoral supervision today, thus drawing out – across the literature and my own empirical studies – the essential aspects of what defines doctoral supervision as a pedagogical phenomenon and event at universities today. Where the majority of research into doctoral supervision, then and now, is based on interviews with supervisors and students, my own research draws on observation of supervision, focusing on the pedagogical and disciplinary meeting between supervisor and student. As will be explained below, the meta-perspective reveals two crucial and essential aspects of doctoral supervision: organization and dialogue.

1.1 Research background

The data material for this book is the result of a two-year double comparative research project, conducted between the fall of 2013 and the fall of 2015, which examined doctoral supervision practices across different institutional levels at the university, from the dean and heads of departments, and the PhD administration, to doctoral supervisors in the specific disciplines and doctoral students. The study relied mainly on observations of doctoral supervision meetings, combined with interviews with the supervisors conducted before and after the meetings. The subject of this qualitative study was the Faculty of Arts at Aarhus University, Denmark. The Humanities Division at the University of Oxford was also used, as a comparative case. The comparative study focused on forms of alignment and diversity with regard to the articulation and understanding of the purpose and pedagogy of doctoral education and supervision across the different institutional levels. Thus, it could be described as doubly comparative: the study examined the understanding of supervision across different institutional levels within individual universities (where Aarhus and Oxford are distinct cases), and across different universities, comparing Aarhus and Oxford.

The literature on doctoral supervision is mainly concerned with how supervisory practices, aligned across different institutional levels, meet the goals of the qualification framework, and how generic skills in managing and organizing doctoral supervision can be developed and perfected. This stands in contrast to the highly contextual and individual pedagogy of doctoral supervision, which cannot easily be contained in a general conceptual vocabulary and framework.

The theoretical framework applied in the analysis was inspired mostly by Lynn McAlpine and Judith Norton's concept of "nested contexts" (McAlpine & Norton 2006; McAlpine & Åkerlind 2010) within doctoral education settings, that is, how different disciplinary, institutional, social and cultural contexts for apprehension, discourse, linguistic habits and codes of conduct all saturate the phenomenon of doctoral supervision simultaneously, entangled and merged within each other. I also drew heavily on Margaret Kiley, Gina Wisker and Gillian Robinson's concept of "crossing conceptual thresholds" (Kiley & Wisker 2009; Wisker & Robinson 2009; Wisker 2012), or how supervisors facilitate the student's approach to and crossing of liminal forms of understanding within the disciplinary context he or she is anchored in. Wisker argues that such conceptual thresholds must be crossed in order to attain the originality, creativity and depth required of a doctoral thesis. Finally, I applied my own concept of "supervisory idiosyncrasy" (Bengtsen 2012; Bengtsen 2011), which I developed in my PhD thesis, based on a study of master's dissertation supervision at Aarhus University. The concept of "supervisory idiosyncrasy" contains the meaning of the situated, individual and highly contextual mode of doctoral supervision practice. These concepts all point to the ambivalence and tension, but also the potential and enrichment, of doctoral supervision as a pedagogical phenomenon that functions on different levels: institutional, disciplinary, and personal.

The book also draws on working papers written during the preparation of the book. Selected material from these working papers have been integrated into the book without further editing. However, during the publication process of the book these working papers have been published independently as Bengtsen 2014a and Bengtsen and Jensen 2015. Whenever material from these, now, publications is being integrated into the text, I quote myself and explicitly cite the passages used.

1.2 Discipline and pedagogy: impossible to separate

During the last seven years of intense research into the nature of master's thesis and doctoral supervision it has become clear to me that, for the supervisor and student, supervision is first and foremost about one thing: the disciplinary context and content. This does not mean that pedagogy and didactics are not important elements of the supervision meeting for the supervisor. It means that pedagogical and didactical dimensions are impossible to separate from the disciplinary content of the dialogue, and that it does not make much sense for supervisors to reflect on their supervisory practice detached from the disciplinary focus. This is not to say that one cannot abstract different elements from the supervisory meeting as Lee (2012; 2008), Gatfield (2005) and Wisker (2012) have done it in their modeling of the supervisory context. And certainly many of the studies mentioned above focus on relational and organizational aspects more than, and at times even apart from, the specific disciplinary content of the supervision meeting. I acknowledge that this can be fruitful in that it allows for the adaptation of approaches for people not themselves working as doctoral supervisors. But honestly, I have difficulty in imagining that supervisors and students themselves can relate to such approaches. As the key aim of this book is to stay focused on the event of doctoral supervision itself, the specific meeting between supervisor and student, and to reflect on other aspects through that event, I intend to give a privileged status to the disciplinary element throughout the book.

However, it is obvious that this is only partially possible as I am not – as researchers into doctoral supervision rarely are – an expert in the fields discussed in the supervision meetings I have studied. Therefore, I try to give voice to the disciplinary content by proxy, putting myself in line with researchers such as McMichael and McKee (2008), who describe doctoral supervision as a special way of teaching disciplinary content, and even the "most complex and subtle form of teaching" (McMichael & McKee 2008: 54) that takes place at the university. In my own work I have tried to tune in to the link between personal-relational and disciplinary elements of supervisory dialogues by showing that "the personal dimension prolongs itself into the very heart of the subject matter at hand in our dialogue. (...) We must understand the personal dimension as a central part of *what* we teach" (Bengtsen 2011: 116-117). Disciplinary content in this context is often linked to the doctoral thesis as an artifact and shared epistemological platform for supervisors and students, as pointed out by Grant (2008) in her emphasis on the fact that relationship building and disciplinary matters in doctoral supervision are almost always "mediated by the thesis", and the supervisor "talks *through* the body of the draft to the student" (Grant 2008: 20).

Certainly, disciplinary content also includes disciplinary communities and their particular worldviews and epistemological vistas and codices. This draws on what is popularly called 'enculturation', which, as I write in my earlier paper (Bengtsen 2014a), "Lee defines as "the process of socialization or acculturation into the discipline, the working milieu (e.g. the academic department and the university) and the national culture". She goes on to state "A person is 'enculturated' when they [...] have learned the traditional content of a culture and assimilated its practices and values" (Lee 2012: 48). As pointed out by many, this understanding of disciplinary content in doctoral supervision settings draws heavily on Wenger's notion of communities of practice – for example in Lee (2012: 51), Wisker (2012: 59) and Peelo (2011: 45), in which supervisors are seen as doctoral students' most important role models, whose ways of working, thinking and even writing are subsequently to some degree adapted by the doctoral students they supervise." (Bengtsen 2014a: 8).

Although the subtitle of the book is "organization and dialogue", the disciplinary content and context is always implicit and always saturates the understanding of the supervision meeting. For instance, when supervisors and students are dealing with organizational matters, formal institutional demands and procedures, they either connect them to core disciplinary arguments or struggle to get it out of the way, so they can get on to what really interests them: the disciplinary content. This is not an endeavor to preach a gospel about disciplinary matters, but to explain that even if disciplinary content may not be directly captured by my terms "organization" and "dialogue", it is always there, as a world or a realm, a force of nature or laws of physics, shaping and bending the organizational and dialogical actions and events. Disciplinary content is the force of gravity that pulls supervision meetings towards their center – whatever that may be, and whatever lies in wait down that path.

1.3 Supervision as organization

The second part of the book (Part II) identifies, defines and discusses one of the two essential elements of doctoral supervision – the organizational element. As a core feature of doctoral supervision, to organize in this context means firstly to give structure to and secondly to facilitate learning processes. The first meaning of organization should be understood as the didactical aspect of doctoral supervision practice, which includes finding and giving a particular logic, order and coherence according to the specific set of rules, expectations and values that belong to the specific scientific and disciplinary paradigm. The second meaning of organization should be understood as the pedagogical aspect of doctoral supervision, which does not focus on finding and giving rules and structure to the content of the supervision meeting, but instead on promoting and facilitating effective processes for learning and developing as a doctoral student, a new researcher, a teacher, a potential member of the staff and as a person more broadly speaking.

Traditionally, in relation to doctoral supervision the term 'organization' is understood as part of the institutional context, which is certainly the case as I see it – but not merely the case. When organization is connected to the institutional context it deals with doctoral supervision as an institutionalized system with formalized procedures about learning goals, work obligations and assessment criteria. Taken up elsewhere (Bengtsen 2014a), "as the conditions for doctoral education change according to a given institutional and educational context, doctoral supervision is very much entangled with the institutional context of the individual university (Peelo 2011: 33-34; Taylor & Beasley 2010: 7ff.; Lee 2012: 31ff.). As the university today is an increasingly public domain, Taylor and Beasley stress that "Research training agendas are being affected by the changes in university-industry-government relationships, adding to the diversity of outcomes that policy makers expect of the doctorate" (Taylor & Beasley 2010: 18). Doctoral education today is not only a matter for the universities to administrate themselves; on the contrary, it is irrevocably "out of the closet and firmly in the public domain, with attendant pressures for responsibility and accountability" (ibid.). With this focus on accountability, the framework for supervision has changed, as Wisker points out: "a new transparency, rigor, and changes in funding have all made a difference to our articulation of the supervision process, and our strategies for evaluating and enhancing it" (Wisker 2012: 57). In relation to supervision, this is intended to provide security to the students and supervisors, enabling a fair and manageable supervision process with regard to the amount of time and resources the student has a right to expect from the supervisor, and vice versa." (Bengtsen 2014a: 6).

In this part of the book I wish to bring attention to the idea that organization is not only about *the* organization, as a noun: that is, the university as an institutional framework. Doctoral supervision is very much about *organizing*, as a verb: organizing a fruitful and stimulating learning environment for the doctoral student to be a part of and to take part in. Noted in my earlier work: "To counter frustration in the long run, Eley and Murray argue for the benefit of a supervisor-facilitated phase of induction in which the student becomes acquainted with the institutional context, codes of conduct and research and workplace ethics (Eley & Murray 2009: 88ff). Induction into this context does not simply mean "introducing the student to the institutional and disciplinary conventions and courses; induction is also a time when supervisors assess students' potential and calculate what type of supervision role they will be required to play" (Eley & Murray 2009: 90). As Delamont, Atkinson and Parry note, such alignment and negotiation of roles between supervisors and students can in itself be called a form of "management" (Delamont, Atkinson & Parry 2004: 14). The way the supervisee is managed may change several times during the process of doctoral supervision of a particular student, and different supervisors choose to approach these issues differently." (Bengtsen 2014a: 7). Induction and management of learning processes and introduction to learning spaces should therefore also be seen as forms of organizing doctoral supervision.

Organizing also covers the supervisor's guidance as to how the thesis fits into the academic and scientific genre, and meets the assessment criteria set forth by international standards. The doctoral student population today has become more heterogeneous, with students from mixed institutional and methodological backgrounds. As argued in my previous work "this has been met with growing research into how supervisors can best advise their doctoral students about acquiring the necessary writing skills to fit their research project into the genre of academia. Lee describes this as "functional supervision", the meaning of which includes the supervisor's "responsibility for identifying a series of milestones that keep the project on track [...]. The functional supervisor and the student are both clear about the assessment criteria that are going to be applied for examining and the requirements for ethical practices are made explicit" (Lee 2012: 30). These guidelines deal primarily with generic skills across the disciplines – the general academic demands of neutrality, objectivity, transparency and coherence of the PhD thesis as an examined product to be handed in and assessed. These guidelines ensure that the thesis is as robust as possible when evaluated and assessed by academics from potentially different disciplines. The supervisor helps the student organize her project through advice and strategies for writing up the thesis, such as that presented in Wisker (2012: 415ff.), and Delamont, Atkinson and Parry (2004: 117ff.); in these examples, guidelines are presented for how supervisors may help their students to pose the right research questions, to structure the text corpus and divide the thesis into sections and chapters and more generally to manage a larger research project. They also cover how to prepare for the viva (PhD defense), which questions to expect and how to engage in an open and critical dialogue with the opponents (Lee 2012: 41; Wisker 2012: 471ff.; Eley & Murray 2009: 118ff.)." (Bengtsen 2014a: 9-10).

I argue that the supervisor's presence in, and relevance to, supervision practice can to a large degree be said to be encompassed by the verb 'to organize'. Many pedagogical and didactical actions take the form of the endeavor to organize or to help the doctoral student organize something. During the supervision meeting supervisors constantly organize the disciplinary content, the research method, the dialogue, the feedback, institutional matters, disciplinary networks and so forth, in conjunction of course with the student. This key feature of doctoral pedagogy has been called by many names, for example 'teaching', 'facilitation', 'instruction', 'induction', 'management' and 'administration'. I argue that these terms do not signify categorically different pedagogical operations, but are different aspects of the same fundamental pedagogical feature that I term 'organization'. To avoid contributing to the trend of making doctoral supervision a highly, maybe even disturbingly, complex and confusing form of pedagogy, I wish to indicate that the meta-term 'organization', or 'organizing', actually covers all of these different subcategories. I acknowledge that doctoral supervision is a very advanced and demanding form of pedagogy, and I do not wish to give the impression that I am downplaying the nuances and contextual nature of the event of the supervision meeting. Neither do I try to "dissolve" the differences between the many various forms of helping the student organize and structure her research project, or argue that you could easily blend all these diverse forms of advice and strategies together into a grey mass labeled 'organizing'. On the contrary, as I will argue in the chapters that follow, the pedagogical interpretation of the verb 'to organize' meets the dynamic, changeable, transformative and highly situational character (McAlpine & McKinnon 2012) that defines doctoral supervision as a specific form of supervision at the university. Organizing doctoral supervision should in this context be heard with overtones of a multilayered pedagogy that acts on many levels at the same time, or, to use the term from McAlpine and Norton (2006), that is nested within many contexts simultaneously.

By using the term 'organization' as a meta-term, or a form of synthesis, I wish to acknowledge that the different layers of doctoral supervision have been well described in literature. However, I argue that in order to define the pedagogical structure of doctoral supervision practice, a term is needed that anchors this diversity in one underlying pedagogical attitude: I have chosen 'organizing', which more fully matches the subtlety and multilayered nature of doctoral supervision practice than any other.

1.4 Supervision as dialogue

The third part of the book (Part III) identifies, defines and discusses the other of the two essential elements of doctoral supervision – the dialogical element. The supervisory dialogue can be defined as an interactive and spontaneous form of communication about a given content, following certain norms of behavior appropriate both socially and to the educational and disciplinary context. The dialogue is the part of the supervision meeting that enables students as well as supervisors to participate in and shape the meeting and the subject matter at hand. The dialogue should be understood as a form of 'technology', a tool that is neutral in nature, and which may be used to make room for, inspire and motivate the doctoral student as well as to dominate, hinder and abuse the student. The dialogue sets doctoral supervision, and supervision at the university more generally, apart from any other learning and teaching format because of its potentially dynamic and highly interactive character compared to other learning and teaching frameworks such as the lecture and classroom teaching. The dialogue is special because it invites negotiated and collaborative work between supervisor and student, and because of the special and oft mentioned conversational intensity and intimacy that results. In doctoral supervision matters the dialogue is used for various purposes such as instruction, teaching, relationship building, feedback, support and motivation.

Made clear in my precious work, "the supervisory dialogue can be said to be part of relationship building due to the key aspects, often linked to the underlying pedagogical foundation, of openness and trust. The supervisory dialogue is most often (in the humanities at least) the primary teaching format available and applied during the doctorate process. Wisker states that supervisory dialogues are "at the heart of the research student's learning" (Wisker 2012: 187). Furthermore, she points out that supervisory dialogues, "whether face-to-face or through electronic means, are the main way in which we work with our students to encourage, direct, support and empower them to get on with and complete their research and writing" (ibid.). The supervisory dialogue is not a classical form of didactics like the tutorial model, but can instead be described as a "learning conversation" and a form of "collaborative problem-solving" (Wisker 2012: 190). Handal and Lauvås underline that most of what we understand as doctoral supervision takes place in the form of conversations between supervisors and students, which can vary from formal and planned meetings with a set agenda to more informal meetings and spontaneous talks in the hallway or by the coffee machine (Handal & Lauvås 2011: 101).

The fact that the dialogue, or conversation, is the primary teaching and learning format poses different forms of challenges for the doctoral supervisor. Given the openness of the dialogue, and the room for spontaneity, non-linear structure and digressions, it can be a challenge to balance the wish for openness and freedom for the student to step forth and to find a voice of his own on the one hand, and the desire to structure the dialogue according to a preset agenda, including e.g. text feedback and other types of comments, on the other. According to Handal and Lauvås, one of the challenges of the supervisory dialogue is that there is no "recipe" or best way to structure it as such, since it is highly dependent on the particular student, supervisor and point in the research process (Handal & Lauvås 2011: 101). Wisker emphasises that the supervisory dialogue is often understood in terms of "play and improvisation" (Wisker 2012: 192), which is mirrored in Peelo's description of supervision as "academic playfulness" (Peelo 2011: 20); the focus is on the potential of the supervisory dialogue as an arena in which students can take risks in their "exploration of ideas and possible avenues of research" (ibid.). No other form of teaching is as fluid and flexible as the supervisory dialogue, which demands a high degree of communicative skill and an ability to 'play' with the disciplinary concepts or frameworks at work in the student's research project." (Bengtsen 2014a: 16-17).

There is a strong consensus in the research literature that the dialogical aspect of supervision is key to understanding the deep pedagogical and epistemological potentials of this form of teaching. However, the dialogue as a teaching format is often taken for granted and not reflected on as one of many possible formats. Dialogue is so closely linked to research supervision, and so strongly anchored in our understanding of doctoral pedagogy and didactics, that we do not question its legitimacy. I wish to make this familiarity of the dialogue unfamiliar by drawing out and discussing some of the implicit pedagogical and epistemological ideals we assume are realized simply by having a dialogue, or series of dialogues, with our students. My aim is to focus on the difficulties, but also great potentials, of 'wielding' the dialogue on an explicit and reflective pedagogical and didactical level. Furthermore, when describing the supervisory dialogue, there is a tendency to view it as something other than and separate from the institutional and formalized aspects of the supervision meeting. The dialogue is seen as a spontaneous and humane dimension that balances the formalized educational framework of the 'system'. I wish to challenge this view and show that the supervisory dialogue is deeply inherent in the institutional set-up, and that dialogue and organization do not oppose but constitute each other. In addition, the dialogue is often described in the literature as a well-rounded whole, robust and dialectical. As will be shown, it is often not so in practice. The dialogue may be said to be 'one' in the sense of a continued and maintained conversation between supervisor and student throughout the supervision meeting. However, it is difficult to say that there is just 'one' dialogue; I shall argue rather that there are many dialogues during a supervision meeting. These different dialogues take place on many levels, and they are not necessarily knotted together. The shifts are constant, sometimes interwoven and sometimes not, and the several 'loose ends' may dangle and be torn to shreds, fragmented and unsolved. These findings call for new and more nuanced ways of understanding and conceptualizing the supervisory dialogue in doctoral supervision pedagogy.

My focus will be set on the implicit ethical and pedagogical ideals inherent in the understanding of dialogue in the Western educational paradigm. In doctoral supervision such ideals have to do especially with the student's hoped for development of autonomy and emancipation in personal, professional and disciplinary matters. As I argue elsewhere, "the research literature agrees on the importance of supervisors supporting and facilitating doctoral students' development of what is referred to as "emancipation", "rational autonomy", "personal development" (Lee 2012: 94-95), "autonomy" and "growth" (Wisker 2012: 108, 191). The students' emancipation is described by Lee as when they "find their own direction and values and [...] decide to apply them to their research" (Lee 2012: 94). Furthermore, Lee stresses that emancipation has a very different objective from enculturation. The academic "who is working within an emancipatory framework will not be seeking to keep their students within the discipline, whereas this will be the prime objective for the academic who is working within the enculturation framework" (ibid.). Wisker links autonomy to the level of originality of research expected of a doctoral student (Wisker 2012: 189), and, in line with Lee, frames it not as personal growth as such, but as the autonomy of the student's research (ibid.). According to Wisker, this poses a challenge for the supervisor to balance and to navigate the tension "between hands-on support and the hands-off encouragement of autonomy, and autonomy which will enable the graduate or postdoc to conduct their own research projects" (Wisker 2012: 189-190)." (Bengtsen 2014a: 11-12).

Delamont, Atkinson and Parry (2004: 34) state that this dilemma has been visible in empirical studies on doctoral supervision as far back as the early 1990s, and that it poses one of the most crucial challenges for doctoral supervisors. Delamont et al. stress that most supervisors experience "a pull between their desire to exercise tight control and to allow the student the freedom that comes from non-interventionist supervision" (ibid.). This point strikes to the heart of a key issue regarding the pedagogy of doctoral supervision. Lee points out that this experience can easily lead to the "dark side" (Lee 2012: 106) of supervision in which the untrained supervisor does not facilitate the autonomous growth of the doctoral student's research project, but instead makes the student work in line with the their own agendas of self-promotion. It can also be difficult to define exactly what autonomous research is, and what personal-professional autonomy looks like. As Wisker writes, this can vary a great deal between educational levels, culturally, contextually (disciplinary), and individually (Wisker 2012: 188). The supervisor should therefore bear in mind that the doctoral student's work must match the level of the degree undertaken, where "greater autonomy and originality are required over a greater length of time for a longer, more significant project, making a contribution to knowledge, and justifying the award of a doctorate" (Wisker 2012: 189).

The supervisory dialogue will be shown to function for supervisors, as well as for students, as a particularly powerful way of listening, referred to as "active listening" (Batchelor 2008; Godskesen & Wichmann-Hansen 2013) and "deep listening" (Brearley & Hamm

2013). In this way the dialogue is used to question, explore, probe and direct the student's argument and mindset, which ideally lets the supervisor understand the student's reflections from 'within' the student's own perspective, or as close to it as is possible in an educational setting. Furthermore, I shall argue that the supervisory dialogue is not 'merely' a conversational and communicative feature, but a critically important way of *thinking* together in a specific setting. As my research shows, this is particularly the case for doctoral supervision where the level of depth and originality is crucial to the success of the endeavor. I shall argue that the learning and research process, the doctoral journey, would be vastly more difficult if dialogue did not provide the fertile and creative thinking environment so essential for epistemological and methodological matters. In conclusion, dialogue will be defined as a magnificent, but also potentially dangerous, technology for supervisors and students to wield. It will be clear that the supervisory dialogue is not one thing, but many, according to the different stages and contexts in which it is applied. It will also be evident that dialogues are highly unruly forms of thinking: sometimes whole and harmonious, sometimes fragmented, broken and torn. As a pedagogical phenomenon it is both wild and controllable, predictable and disturbingly unpredictable, presenting a serious task for the supervisor at every single supervision meeting. Dialogue is something we undertake, but it is also something that happens *to* us.

1.5 Advanced pedagogy

The fourth, and final, part of the book (Part IV) hones in on new challenges for future research and the need for further developmental work in doctoral supervision. This part highlights key findings from my own research, which discovers things that cannot be contained by traditional concepts and frameworks of meaning, but demand the development of new concepts for doctoral supervision pedagogy. I treat five essential aspects of doctoral supervision that all contribute to and define it as a particularly advanced form of pedagogy.

The first essential aspect that emerges from my observation studies is that doctoral supervision may be said to be a specific form of 'ambivalent pedagogy'. As noted by Handal and Lauvås, doctoral supervision often includes both a product and a process dimension (e.g. Handal & Lauvås 2011: 58-59). The process dimension usually covers the collaborative and explorative features of the supervisory dialogue, in which supervisor and student work more together to get a grasp on an issue brought forth by the student as being particularly challenging in the work process. As stated in my previous work, "the product dimension covers advice and strategies for writing up the thesis, such as that presented in Wisker (2012: 415ff.), and Delamont, Atkinson and Parry (2004: 117ff.); in these examples, guidelines are presented for how supervisors may help their students to pose the right research questions, structure the text corpus and divide the thesis into sections and chapters and more generally to manage a larger research project." (Bengtsen 2014a: 10). Product supervision is an asymmetrical dialogue in which the supervisor evaluates the student's work and gives feedback for improvement. The ambivalence that became visible in my observations is that the supervisor and student take very different roles in the two forms of supervision, and that these forms of pedagogy did not always seem to complement each other as intended; in fact, they could be seen to work against each other, eroding the intended learning outcome.

Secondly, doctoral supervision can be thought of as a 'subtle pedagogy'. My observations show that during a single meeting it is not uncommon that several 'sub-meetings' take place, characterizing the overall event as meetings within meetings within meetings. One meeting may hold sub-meetings about institutional matters, disciplinary and knowledge based issues to be addressed, how to structure the research process and issues regarding the overall learning process that students usually bring to the fore in one way or another. As I argue elsewhere, "the supervisor is not only, as Wisker points out, "a complex, professional, personal and political role" (Wisker 2012: 59); they also have to balance their own work pressures, specific departmental administrative and economical challenges, while assisting the doctoral student to navigate the same institutional layout, though from a different level of expertise. Peelo notes that this complexity can become, for both supervisor and student, an "intellectually complex experience and one that [...] provides both supervisors and students with plenty of opportunities for miscommunication and misunderstanding" (Peelo 2011: 48)." (Bengtsen 2014a: 6-7). Grant makes a similar point, stating that precisely because doctoral supervision pedagogy takes place as a multilayered event, the contact and the basis for mutual understanding is fraught with a certain form of pedagogical "slipperiness" (Grant 2006: 338). This aligns well with the notion mentioned before about doctoral supervision consisting of several "nested contexts" (McAlpine & Norton 2006) internally intertwined in sometimes beneficial and sometimes more chaotic ways. This suggests just how many potential pitfalls are present during each meeting, calling for more attention to the exceedingly subtle pedagogy demanded in successful doctoral supervision.

Thirdly, when observed closely and intensively, doctoral supervision pedagogy contains elements that are not easy, perhaps even not possible, to pin down as general aspects of doctoral supervision at all. Such aspects of teaching and learning have elsewhere been termed "strange" (Barnett 2007) or "weird" (Bengtsen & Nørgård 2014), meaning that they do not abide by the same pedagogical 'laws of nature' as can be found in other settings of a similar type. As shown in my PhD thesis (Bengtsen 2012), supervision meetings are often highly labyrinthine in character, taking detours and straying from the preset agenda stated by the supervisor at the beginning of the meeting. The intellectual spaces unfolded by supervisor and student are not always aligned, and they may seem to end up in different places during the dialogue, so that they have difficulty in finding each other again and getting back on track. In such instances the observations show that supervisor and student 'search' for each other in thought and language, often being reunited on the same, but not predicted and planned, platform of meaning somehow. How they got there, and how they lost each other in the first place, can pedagogically speaking be quite hard to explain, as the intellectual space, or thinking space, is so much a personal, even idiosyncratic (Bengtsen 2012; Bengtsen 2011) phenomenon. This points to doctoral supervision as being a particularly strange form of pedagogy.

Fourthly, out of my studies arises an aspect of doctoral supervision pedagogy I call 'embedded pedagogy'. Doctoral supervision pedagogy is embedded within the disciplinary content discussed by supervisor and student to such a degree that it can be difficult for supervisors themselves, as well as researchers, to pin down clearly what the pedagogical act consists of. When supervisors guide or direct a student in relation to a specific question the student asks, this embedded nature becomes present in two ways. Firstly the student's question may often concern the learning process in general, but is addressed by the student as a question framed within a disciplinary horizon of certain disciplinary-epistemological issues. The supervisor meets such questions with a language steeped in the terminology of the discipline, though later in the interview they made clear that the problem concerned learning issues, not merely disciplinary concerns. This understanding of doctoral supervision as an embedded form of pedagogy draws in particular on the work done by Gina Wisker, Margaret Kiley and Gill Robinson (Wisker & Robinson 2009; Kiley & Wisker 2009; Wisker 2012), analyzing doctoral supervision through the lens of 'crossing conceptual thresholds', an idea originally promoted by Ray Land, Jan H.F. Meyer and Jan Smith (2008).

The final aspect I wish to draw attention to is doctoral supervision as a particular kind of 'torn' pedagogy. I use this term to draw out the different conditions, possibilities and challenges of net-based doctoral supervision. Doctoral supervision takes place using many different online platforms, e.g. Skype, Google Hangouts, Google Docs and regular email, in which feedback is often given using review functions in documents sent back and forth between supervisor and student. Interestingly this well-known and everyday practice has not been thoroughly studied or even described in the literature on doctoral supervision. As detailed elsewhere (Bengtsen & Mathiasen 2014; Bengtsen, Mathiasen & Dalsgaard 2015; Bengtsen & Jensen 2015), the pedagogy and media used for supervision are deeply linked, and the conditions for presence, trust, dialogue and feedback are transformed when mediated by online platforms and tools. One of the conditions I discuss is the supervisors' feeling, imagined or real, of the pedagogy and teaching becoming more fragmented and kaleidoscopic, lacking the strong center of the face-to-face meeting. Net-based doctoral supervision also allows for abundant feedback with a high degree of diversity that it is not possible to provide in the same way in face-to-face supervision. I use the term 'torn' to represent traditional doctoral supervision being torn to shreds, transformed and rebuilt in online forums, giving the unique form of pedagogy a new, challenging but also promising character.

In the final part of the book I define key aspects of doctoral supervision pedagogy that, together with the overall terms 'organization' and 'dialogue', stipulate essential conditions and challenges for doctoral supervisors to be mindful of:

- Ambivalent pedagogy
- Subtle pedagogy
- Strange pedagogy
- Embedded pedagogy
- Torn pedagogy

Together, these aspects form a definition of doctoral supervision as an 'advanced pedagogy' that requires new concepts and terminology for it to be acknowledged and practiced in its full potential. Laying bare these different advanced features of doctoral supervision, with the intention of providing doctoral supervisors with concepts and language to feed into their own reflections about their supervision practices, calls for new approaches in future doctoral supervision research. Such research must be equally subtle and diverse in order to meet the subtlety and diversity in doctoral supervision practice. New forms of research must supplement the observation studies and interview studies that have been carried out so far. They could be done in more thorough collaboration with doctoral supervisors and students; they could also follow more closely the entire three-year (or more) PhD process to see how the roles, relations and forms of organization and dialogue change throughout the different phases of the PhD, as well as the different contexts, including learning and teaching environments, the supervision becomes part of. This leads to my final conclusion about doctoral supervision as a multiform, hard to pin down in both nature and format, but with an essence, or essence-like, quality that defines its pedagogy as an entirely autonomous and specific type, which must be understood on its own terms and in its own right.

PART 2
SUPERVISION AS ORGANIZATION

Common to all institutions, departments, supervisors and students when engaged in doctoral education and supervision is the endeavor of organizing teaching and learning. The following chapter describes the many different ways we organize, and the many shapes and forms organization may take. When we organize we give structure, we mold, model and form, we find platforms and plateaus and, perhaps most fundamentally, we give value and meaning to the PhD.

This chapter aims to clarify what organizing doctoral supervision means, and to lay bare the different levels of organization that influence, condition and support the doctoral supervisor and student in their joint endeavor. Organizing takes place on many different levels in the institution at the same time, as well as in arenas other than the institution, as a fenced-in physical and social place. Often the term 'institutional context' has been used in a narrow way to define institutional matters as forms of qualification, criteria for assessment, and standards for supervisors' and students' tasks and responsibilities (Taylor & Beasley 2010; Phillips & Pugh 2012). In this narrow sense, the 'institution' is contrasted with terms like 'the disciplinary context' and 'informal contexts'.

This chapter argues that several learning and thinking spaces constitute an institutional context, some formalized, some deeply tacit and cloaked in the hub and murmur of everyday disciplinary practice, some entirely removed from the institution as a place. What can be said to be common to all of them is that their organization is about giving value, meaning and purpose to doctoral education and supervision, sometimes by applying structure and systems, sometimes by building cultures and establishing norms and habits that make it easier, or harder, for the doctoral student to find a footing and to model his or her own thinking and work processes. In this chapter, which is based on findings from my research project and studies of the research literature, I argue that five essential educational features define doctoral supervision as organization: (1) formal organization; (2) enculturation, or informal organization; (3) non-formal organization; (4) thesis organization, and (5) roles and relations as organizers.

2.0 FORMAL ORGANIZATION

Formal organization in doctoral supervision can be said to occur in three different types of formalization: system, induction, and contract. These three types define the ways that supervisors and students understand and give meaning to formalizing features they experience as influencing the context of their supervision meetings. However, my study also showed that supervisors and students are ambivalent about such formalization. Supervisors and students simultaneously call for more clarification and overt structure and procedures for support during the PhD *and* they experience and articulate formalizing aspects as sources of irritation and frustration, as they disturb the PhD process and sometimes divert the supervisory dialogue into non-disciplinary and less relevant areas.

2.0.1 System

The aspect of 'system' in doctoral supervision encompasses the professionalization of the supervision task that has become particularly influential in most universities worldwide during the last decade. Before professionalization was set on the agenda in higher education developmental programs, many doctoral supervisors experienced that "as university professors, we learned to supervise 'on the fly', learning by doing. We used each other as sounding boards and discovered that we shared similar experiences" (McMichael & McKee 2008: 54). As a solution to this more random and unsupported learning process, the advent of professionalization has formalized aspects of doctoral education, such as how to advise students on writing up their thesis (Murray 2011; Trafford & Leshem 2012); how to assess the doctoral thesis (Pearce 2004; Tinkler & Jackson 2004); and how to guide and prepare doctoral students for the viva (Murray 2009; Morley, Leonard & David 2010). However, as Manathunga (2005) points out, such forms of professionalization are sometimes carried out as "mandatory programs that may solely focus on the administrative roles and responsibilities of supervisors, attempting to provide technical 'fixes' that deny the genuine difficulties and complexities involved in supervision relationships" (Manathunga 2005: 17).

This has been experienced and interpreted by many supervisors as "further instances of the quality assurance agendas of governments and university administrators", which has made them "suspicious of what some describe as the colonial underpinnings of educational development" (ibid.). Such programs for supervisor development often focus on employment outcomes, explicit skills formation and timely completion (Pearson & Brew 2002). Unfortunately, systems that are intended to help supervisors and students alike, by making visible and managing the formal structures and goals of doctoral education, are often felt as a heightened pressure by the supervisors themselves (ibid.). Pearson and Brew mention that supervisors feel the pressure to ensure "student throughput, be more flexible in an open system and provide students with more support" (Pearson & Brew 2002: 136). Such systems in many ways seem to present a double-edged sword, exposing gaps between different levels of policy making, administration and supervision practice in the organizational structure.

The underlying logic of the system is based, for good and for worse, on the premise that good supervision emerges out of clear and preset learning goals, learning outcomes and learning management. This aspect of formalization rests on the assumption and belief that supervision processes can be messy and spin out of control, so they should be tamed and rationalized into procedures and contracts. In this understanding of doctoral supervision students are met with guidance about "managing influences of personal circumstances" and "managing your skills development" (Cryer 2006), as well as warnings to "be aware that you must accept the responsibility for managing the relation between you and your supervisors. It is too important to be left to chance" (Phillips & Pugh 2012: 108). Supervisors are warned that doctoral students are fragile beings, like butterflies that might be "caught and held by a cobweb" (Delamont,

Atkinson & Parry 2004: 14). Lee connects this aspect of formalization with what she calls "functional teaching and supervision" and links it to a "managerial approach" (Lee 2012: 31). The underlying logic of the system in doctoral supervision settings is described by Grant as "a matter of technical rationality" (Grant 1999: 2), a perspective that is "attractive, particularly to university bureaucracies (and their funding bodies) who want predictable outcomes and timely completion" (ibid). In an ideal world, the system is used by supervisors and students to prepare for the unexpected and to keep students on the right track by inviting them to document and reflect on their research and learning processes throughout the PhD.

The system as a formalizing aspect of doctoral supervision was part of all of the supervision meetings observed. At the Faculty of Arts at Aarhus University, a program called 'PhD Planner' is used to keep track of individual doctoral students' progression. The program is supported by the Graduate School at the Faculty of Arts, and the supervisors use the program partly to keep track of the students' learning processes and partly to report and document their progression for the Graduate School. The system was used as a tool for the supervisors and students alike to organize the formal dimension of the students' research projects. In supervision meetings, it functioned as a way to archive central elements of the student's work processes, but also to make visible any gaps, and any needs the student might have in terms of further support. In addition, it made these needs clear in environments outside the supervisory dyad.

An interesting observation was that supervisors, and students to a lesser degree, used their own 'manual' system of keeping track of the doctoral project by use of computer documents, and some used notebooks solely or in combination with computer documents. Firstly, this shows that keeping and maintaining a system seems to be important, especially for supervisors, to reduce and manage the complexity of the large scale and multifaceted nature of the PhD project. Secondly, this shows that supervisors, and students to a lesser degree, experience a distance between the Graduate School's system and their own personal, or 'local', systems. This corresponds with Manathunga's findings, that the system is a central and necessary way of organizing, but there also exists a need to create, maintain and operate systems on a more "local" level (Manathunga 2005: 21). This suggests that the aspects of system need to be understood and discussed in a more nuanced manner in future supervisor developmental work, and to be accepted as a central way of organizing supervision meetings and PhDs more generally. Instead of linking the system one-sidedly to a large organizational body, we should talk about different systems, and how they can be linked across organizational levels.

Another interesting thing about the system is the ambivalence that it seems to inspire in both supervisors and students. During the interviews and follow-up conversations supervisors and students alike described the system as a two-sided phenomenon. On the one hand they felt the system to be a disturbing element in their supervision meetings, and often a cause of irritation and frustration as it diverted their attention and focus away from the research dimension to what they felt were administrative parts of the process. Both students and supervisors also expressed a rather skeptical attitude to the mandatory PhD courses arranged and administrated by the Graduate School. These courses, which are mostly about how to teach and supervise in higher education, were felt to be remote from the disciplinary field of the individual doctoral student, part of a different system that was less relevant and more alien. On the other hand, supervisors and students both expressed the need for more overt support from departmental and other organizational levels, for when students experienced personal or health problems or other non-disciplinary, practical matters influenced the supervision process.

Based on my observations, the system can be said to represent a door in and out of the more private, or local, space of the supervision meeting, as a reminder that there are obligations and tasks to be fulfilled elsewhere, but also options and possibilities to pursue outside the supervisory dyad. In some meetings the system seemed to hover over the meeting and cast an ever-present shadow. And sometimes the system seemed to lift the meeting by giving it focus and thus a freedom to think more freely after the practical and administrative things had been dealt with. My observations led me to conclude, as supervisors and students did in the interviews, that the system can be seen as a neutral 'technology' – at times working as a disturbing and menacing aspect, and at times serving as a memory bank, helping supervisors and students to keep (on) track, both to remember and to look ahead to the tasks awaiting them in the coming phases of the supervision process. At other meetings the system served as a 'storeroom' or an attic, in which things could be put away – with the danger that they might disappear, but also sometimes supervisors and students found important things they had forgotten when looking for other things in the system.

Instead of being understood as a one-sided monitoring aspect for formalizing doctoral supervision and education, the system should be seen as a plastic pedagogical tool or method with which supervisors and students alike can, if only momentarily and with the intention of breaking free afterwards, frame the supervision meeting and supervision process more generally. The system can be a shelter for students to take cover in when the research process becomes too complex to wield, or for supervisors to step back and get an overview of the students' plans in order to give more relevant and focused feedback. The system is not merely a way of forcing a dynamic and vibrant research process into a rigid schema, but also a safe haven and a plateau from which the entire valley of research can be scanned from a distance.

2.0.2 Induction and formalized learning environments

The second aspect of organization considered here is induction and the formalization of learning environments surrounding the doctoral supervision meetings. As mentioned in the introduction, 'induction' refers to the formalized procedures of welcoming and introducing doctoral students to the disciplinary and departmental environment in which they are working, as well as integrating them. Induction differs from enculturation as it is formalized, with overt and explicitly defined and systematized procedures. As described by Eley and Murray (2009: 88ff.), the aspect of induction involves presenting the new doctoral student with the departmental and disciplinary expectations and the opportunities for support and help available. According to Lee (2012), the supervisor is also encouraged to use the phase, or pedagogical act, of induction to "assess the student and the type of supervision that they will most benefit from" (Lee 2012: 39). Induction is traditionally linked to the initial phase of the PhD, but afterwards doctoral supervisors and students are found to be employing a range of different strategies to formalize and overtly facilitate learning and environments that are assumed to be helpful in countering intellectual and social isolation and other signs associated with students dropping out.

Induction can be achieved, as suggested by Delamont, Atkinson and Parry (2004: 16), with handbooks that specifically address doctoral students and which build on experiences from former students. Cryer (2006) reminds us that "research degrees are seldom failed. In general, students either pass them or simply drop out and have their registration terminated. Causes of drop-out normally lie either in lack of the right motivation (...) or in personal circumstances which do not permit the work to be given the attention it requires." (Cryer 2006: 94-95). To overcome isolation and to maintain momentum and improve motivation during the PhD, Taylor and Beasley (2010) suggest that supervisors help students develop certain "self-management skills" (Taylor & Beasley 2010: 111), such as seeing the PhD as a professional work to be done and not as an overwhelming quest for the Holy Grail.

Another strategy that echoes across much of the literature about doctoral supervision is the formalization of support for doctoral students to develop study groups between themselves. Boud and Lee (2005) suggest using peer environments as a form of induction and self-management, and that "peer learning (...) situated within a notion of communities of research practice, might be a productive frame through which to view research education" (Boud & Lee 2005: 501). Dysthe and Samara (2006) argue that peer disciplinary communities should be seen as an important and often overlooked arena of doctoral supervision, and propose that such collective peer supervision arenas "outside" the traditional supervision dyad between one supervisor and one student should be formalized to a higher degree than is normally the case. In line with Dysthe and Samara, Philips and Pugh argue for the need for organized self-help and peer support groups, or "buddy systems" as they call them (Philips & Pugh 2012: 104), which can also be performed and facilitated online in "internet groups" (Philips & Pugh 2012: 105). The advantage of these online formats is that they can reduce isolation and promote the establishment of relevant disciplinary contact between doctoral students who do not belong to the same department, university or country. Petre and Rugg (2011) underline the importance of building networks and call attention to the fact that "networks don't just happen; they're something you build" (Petre & Rugg 2011: 59). Petre and Rugg also provide suggestions for how to initiate contact between doctoral peers, and they see the forming of networks as a task for the supervisor to facilitate: they point out that "at the heart of your network, of course, are your supervisors" (ibid.). What is crucial across all the different forms of formalized learning environments is that they are, at least initially, facilitated by supervisors, and sometimes even driven by and dependent on them.

The underlying rationale and purpose of induction and formalized learning environments is firstly that the supervisor takes on the role of the host while the student assumes the role of the guest when beginning his or her PhD. After the induction phase the student is no longer considered a 'guest' but a more regular member of the department. When speaking of induction, it must be remembered that the point is not about including doctoral students in communities of practice, but about formally and overtly organizing their first stage of the PhD in a way that mitigates the difficulties of beginning such a large project. Secondly, the purpose is to address the colleague/student schism often experienced by doctoral students, as they are addressed alternately by members of staff as colleagues and as students. By raising these issues formally, the supervisor may help new doctoral students facing the challenge of finding his or her footing within the department. Thirdly, the purpose is to lay the ground for self-management and the establishing of support groups and buddy systems between doctoral students, which indicates the ultimate purpose of induction – that is, to make its own organizing action unnecessary.

During my observations of doctoral supervision meetings it was interesting to see how the supervisors 'nudged' their students to develop certain arguments or parts of their thesis further by discussing them with other students, or in a colloquium or seminar in a mixed group of peers. As supervisors cannot always monitor the changes students make after the feedback is received, they sometimes express a hope that their students will seek out peer groups to gain more perspectives on their work, and to be inspired by the work of others. Though this 'nudging' occurred during most of the observed supervision meetings, the supervisors rarely offered direct support to facilitate such peer groups, but seemed to expect that the students themselves would take care of it. Of course this could be interpreted as the supervisors trusting their students and making space for their emancipation and growth as individual researchers. However, it could alternatively show the supervisors being somewhat reluctant to take on the responsibility of helping their students set up such groups, because of concerns about the extra time and energy they would need to devote to it 'outside' their supervision practice.

During the interviews both the supervisors and students called for more formalized facilitation of learning environments outside the supervision meetings. Both groups also wished that the induction phase had been carried out more thoroughly, in terms of involving more staff and organizational levels so that the students could be made aware of all the resources available to them during the PhD. Supervisors and students also called for more overt and formalized facilitation of student support groups and arenas for peer supervision. Not that they doubted the independence of the students, but both groups still saw that support was needed in the initial phases of building such groups and networks. During the interviews the supervisors and students on the one hand wished for more formalization of induction, but at the same time refrained from placing the responsibility in the hands of the Graduate School of the faculty, which was thought of as being somewhat removed from the departments. Instead the supervisors and students wished for a more local process of formalization of peer support in the disciplinary and departmental arenas. This pointed to a recurring tension between formal and informal organization that is not easy to solve.

During the supervision meetings, peer support groups were seen to be kept as a backdoor option for supervisors and students. If discussions were going in circles or otherwise becoming tiresome, they could be more easily dissolved by supervisors, or in some cases by the students themselves, by hinting that the student should maybe look further into this or that later on – and get more feedback from other sources, for example peers or other members of the staff. It can also be argued that because peer support groups and networks are kept in the hinterland somewhere outside the specific supervision meeting, the present meeting can be more focused. Because the supervision meeting did not have to deal with issues of motivation, momentum and writing difficulties – unless they were pressing, in which case it was of course taken up and dealt with by the supervisor – they could be kept in the periphery, and the meeting could delve into other and more central 'disciplinary-heavy' issues.

The aspect of formalized learning environments outside the supervision meeting can be seen as an organizer in the sense that supervisors use such support groups and networks, whether actual or potential, as a buffer. That is, the supervisors, and to a lesser extent the students, could 'push' certain challenges in the project slightly to the side, to be dealt with further in other arenas. It could also be seen as a way of creating a hierarchy of issues, from issues that need attention from the supervisor themselves to issues that could be dismissed to other forums. This was never viewed as the supervisor being abusive or arrogant for refusing to deal with such issues, but as a way of creating different supervision 'spaces' for the student, allowing for other, multiple potential supervision spaces. Some supervisors explicitly used this strategy to make their students aware that supervision could be seen as a 'plastic' phenomenon, something that takes place in different forums, and which can be facilitated by other students or members of staff, as well as supervisors.

2.0.3 Contract

The third aspect of formalized organization is that of the contract. During the PhD, contracts and mutual alignments of expectations between doctoral supervisors and students take many forms, but they share the feature of mutual agreement. As Grant (1999) states, contracts are often used as a means of eliminating potential misunderstandings and failures of communication between supervisors and students, or to solve problems already existing in the supervisory dyad. Contracts may be oral, written, tacit, assumed or implied. As an aspect of formalized organization I deal only with the written contract. Contracts serve both as formal and informal documents that make specific agreements and expectations regarding the supervision process explicit. Across the literature contracts have been described in various ways, from Lee's description of "Gantt charts" as a "spreadsheet showing all the tasks with their start and finish dates on a time line" (Lee 2012: 43), to Eley and Murray's "meeting logs" that can be "a useful tool for recording the outcome of regular informal meetings" and as "documentary evidence showing proof of meetings (...) in cases of student complaints of inadequate supervision" (Eley & Murray 2009: 77-78). In addition, Cryer states that contracts can "ease anxiety by externalizing what has to be done so that it need not be constantly occupying one's mind" and can "provide a basis for reflection so that future planning can be more realistic" (Cryer 2006: 130).

On the basis of empirical studies Handal and Lauvås conclude that the importance of contracts in doctoral supervision depends on how actively they have been integrated into doctoral supervision meetings (Handal & Lauvås 2011: 30). They also point out that studies conducted at the University of Bergen in Norway showed that when contracts were applied in doctoral supervision, students completed their PhDs one semester earlier (ibid.). Wisker (2012) speaks of "learning contracts" as means for the doctoral student to become more aware of the work lying ahead and the responsibilities he or she might face. She writes that "contracts focus on terms of work, communication and responsibility. As you discuss your roles and draw up an informal or more formal contract, it helps make explicit your expectations, frequency and kind of supervision, and what to avoid" (Wisker 2012: 92). Although much has been written about the use of contracts in doctoral supervision, it is difficult not to foreground Hockey's classic study (Hockey 1996). Hockey is well aware that the contract may unintentionally lead to more "student dependency on the supervisor" (Hockey 1996: 367), and that contracts, when written down, may cause unwanted rigidity and "inflexibility" in the supervision process (ibid.). However, for him the real force of the contract is as an act of mutual agreement and obligation, which "reflects a situation in which there is mutual interest in achieving a common objective – the progress of the thesis" (Hockey 1996: 365). From this perspective, the contract is not interesting so much because of its semi-legal or managerial side effects, but because it makes explicit that "within the context of a supervisory relationship, the consideration of both supervisor and student will commit them to certain duties and responsibilities" (ibid.).

A similar point is made by Halse and Malfroy (2010), who describe this relation between supervisor and student as "the learning alliance". This alliance is "the agreement between supervisor and student to work on a common goal, namely the production of a high quality doctorate" (Halse & Malfroy 2010: 83). Halse and Malfroy also use the term "contract" to define the nature of the learning alliance, stating that "the learning alliance is a contract between supervisor and student, and is akin to the collaborative 'therapeutic alliance' between a patient and clinician" (ibid.). This parallel emphasizes the relational aspects of trust, responsibility and mutual commitment.

In this sense the contract functions as a relational constituent. Its rationale and purpose is to introduce a 'third party', a neutral platform between supervisor and student, from which both can speak. At the same time the contract safeguards and gives physical form to the mutual commitment between supervisor and student. This, as Hockey perceptively notes, is not the same as the system, because the essence of the contract is not the managerial dimension. Instead, it is a way of formalizing a mutual agreement between supervisor and student that is essentially of a relational character.

In the observed supervision meetings the contract figured as a central element and pedagogical tool, both to demarcate milestones and to maintain the flow and progression of the supervisory dialogue. It was used by supervisors and students to reach joint conclusions about the nature of the student's progress. This was typically done when the supervisor, against the backdrop of the student's reflections about his or her progress, wrote down a line or two to make the joint understanding manifest. When these minor 'milestones' had been 'formally' noted, the supervisory dialogue could move on to the next issue. In this way the contract, the written mutual agreement on the status quo of the process, served a summative *and* formative function regarding the flow of the supervisory dialogue. In contrast to the literature on the subject, my observations showed that during supervision meetings the idea of the contract has a more fragmented nature than has formerly been described. Contracts can also be said to include more varied forms of written agreements between supervisor and student. Some forms of contract were written down; on paper, in computer documents, on post-its or in the margin of the student's draft material presented for feedback. Some contracts were constituted orally, and some by email or in more informal departmental communication environments online. These many different mutual agreements on the status of the research process often served as a kind of glue during the observed supervision meetings, in that they simultaneously functioned as a way of summing up, of looking forward, and of making new stages of the commitment between supervisor and student tangible and materially manifest.

The contract can be said to constitute a 'third space' existing between the supervisor and student. This did not depend, in the observed meetings, on it being formally written down and signed or even being more informally drafted and agreed upon orally. The contract can thus be said, on some level, to be about a symbolic act of looking each other in the eyes, shaking hands and giving each other one's word that they are still committed to the supervision process. To build on Hockey's work, the contract can in this sense be seen as building a raft or a bond between parties in a murky grey zone between the personal and professional dimensions of the supervision process. To facilitate this difficult professional-personal commitment the contract may prove beneficial as a tool or instrument to establish and maintain a neutral third space. This discloses a rather paradoxical feature of the contract: though contracts are often material products they serve as process tools to facilitate and organize the dynamic and flow of supervision meetings.

During the supervision meetings the contract was often used as a way of holding the supervision process together. This was done with remarks such as: "As we agreed upon in our last meeting...", and "If you work further on these data, we may be able to conclude something more specific at our next meeting". Such references to earlier or future contracts served as points to steer from, and paths to follow or former journeys to reflect on. Contracts may in this light be seen as signposts, or maps: navigation points to look for and plateaus to be reached, when the overall structure needs to be readdressed and future steps need to be agreed upon. It is important to stress the process element of contracts. Some contracts were observed to be made but then soon forgotten, or lost, as they served more as a way of carrying the process onwards than as a joint memory. The key issue when forming contracts, which is also captured by Wisker and Hockey, is the learning potential for the student. Each time a contract is formed the student is confronted with the status quo of his or her project and the probable implications for future work. Therefore, the essence of the contract is not a finished and signed document, but the process of drawing it up and reflecting on the implications of its content for the next step in the research project.

2.1 ENCULTURATION – INFORMAL ORGANIZATION

Enculturation, or informal organization and learning, covers the part of doctoral supervision and education that cannot easily be formalized and made explicit. Terms like 'tacit knowledge' and 'communities of practice' often cling to the meaning of enculturation, and in this aspect it differs from formalized ways of organizing doctoral supervision. However, enculturation is very much a part of the institutional layout, and it is often obvious and reflexive for the supervisors and students within the particular disciplines. In other words, enculturation is a more discipline-specific dimension of doctoral supervision. In contrast to non-formal organization, described below, enculturation is within the radar, and not below the radar or in a blind spot as often is the case with non-formal organization. It is thus similar to formalized organization in the way that it is used actively and consciously by supervisors and students in supervision processes, though it is similar to non-formal organization in that it is hard to make generic and explicit across particular contexts.

Enculturation contains certain challenges, as described by Nita Cherry (2012), when doctoral supervisors and students experience supervisory matters to attain a certain foggy and paradoxical character. Cherry argues that supervisors should pay more attention to the "knowing, doing, being and becoming of practitioners and not simply their skills, knowledge, tools of trade or the formal learning processes" (Cherry 2012: 8). She highlights the often obscured challenges and the implications this creates for aspects of knowledge creation and relationship building in the supervisory dyad or team. In contrast to the formalized aspects of doctoral supervision, Cherry claims that supervisors and students often find themselves in "foggy territory" (Cherry 2012: 11) when issues in their relationship cannot be managed by formalized procedures only, and when socio-cultural norms and personal values determine the outcome of an otherwise professional practice.

2.1.1 Role models and paradigms

Important parts of doctoral supervision take place as 'role modeling'. On more implicit or tacit levels the doctoral student learns about organization, the research field, academic craftsmanship and research designs by observing how their supervisor talks, acts and handles issues in the academic community. This is usually referred to as the 'informal' dimension of doctoral supervision practice. Philips and Pugh stress that role modeling "is a very important aspect of your task as supervisor. It is not a case of saying 'do as I tell you' but more a case of students gradually learning to 'do as you do', whether that is what you prefer or not" (Philips & Pugh 2012: 191). In this process the doctoral student, sometimes explicitly and sometimes tacitly, learns and assimilates the supervisor's disciplinary "world view", as Wisker calls it (Wisker 2012: 173): the way the supervisor 'sees' the world of her discipline and how she acts according to the norms and habits of thought and conduct.

Building on Aristotle's concept of *phronesis*, Halse and Malfroy (2010) call this the supervisor's "habit of mind", the way that she expresses organizational and disciplinary know-how, a "lived knowledge that enables individuals to exercise deliberative reasoning to make considered judgments about how to act in particular situations to bring about positive change" (Halse & Malfroy 2010: 85). On the individual level this form of enculturation can be connected to a mutual adaptation by the doctoral supervisor and student to each other's "thinking styles" (Sternberg 2010). Though this is a two-way street, the position of the learner means the student absorbs more from the supervisor in act and thought than the other way round. This explains why the relationship between supervisor and student is usually thought of not as symmetrical, as pointed out by Wisker (Wisker 2012: 49), but as asymmetrical, as in the case of the master–apprentice relationship.

On the social level this aspect of organization is often described, based on work by Lave and Wenger (Pearson & Brew 2002: 142), as how the doctoral student becomes part of a specific community of practice, and is socialized to become a scholar (Gardner & Mendoza 2010; Golde & Walker 2006; Walker et al 2008). In the words of Becher and Trowler (2001), this process means the doctoral student becomes part of the academic tribe; Delamont, Atkinson and Parry (2000) describe it from a sociological angle influenced by Bourdieu, focusing on the different cultures of the academy. As I described in my previous work, "Lee (2012; 2008) defines enculturation as "the process of socialization or acculturalisation into the discipline, the working milieu (e.g. the academic department and the university) and the national culture. A person is 'enculturated' when they [...] have learned the traditional content of a culture and assimilated its practices and values" (Lee 2012: 48). Empirical studies show that academics identify themselves by their discipline first and by their department or university second (ibid.). As pointed out by Lee (2012: 51), Wisker (2012: 59) and Peelo (2011: 45), this understanding draws especially on Wenger's work on communities of practice, in which supervisors are seen as doctoral students' most important role models, whose ways of working, thinking and even writing are to some degree adopted by the doctoral students they supervise. However, as Delamont, Atkinson and Parry argue (2004: 182), this is a two-way street: just as doctoral students look to their supervisors for examples of appropriate conduct, supervisors look to their doctoral students for the signs of a good future researcher in the specific discipline they represent.

It is acknowledged across the literature that enculturation is a powerful dimension of influence in the individual doctoral student's path to becoming an academic. However, as enculturation is mostly a tacit phenomenon operating in the hinterland of formal doctoral education, its potential is fraught with challenges and potential conflict. Cultural habits and values tacitly grounded within the disciplines can be difficult to appreciate, especially for students coming from other disciplines or national and cultural contexts. To counter these issues, Lee (2012: 58) suggests ten ways to facilitate student socialization in the discipline. She points to many similar situations throughout the disciplines used to encourage enculturation, such as "doctoral students giving seminars or papers to each other and to members of the department, inviting and organizing external speakers to give seminars and attending conferences [...]" (Lee 2012: 53); other examples include writing independent journal articles or co-writing them with veteran academics in the field. Furthermore, Dysthe and Samara (2006; see also Mullen and Tuten 2010) focus explicitly on the value of teams as a resource in relation to doctoral supervision, either peer groups or supervisor facilitated groups. They claim that an important strategy for success in enculturation is striving for formalization, thereby enabling the disciplinary community with a new, formal and explicated role in supervision practice (Dysthe & Samara 2006: 11). In line with Dysthe and Samara, Handal and Lauvås (2011) point to the changed conditions for supervision strategies and pedagogies in the use of groups as a teaching format in contexts of doctoral supervision. Supervising in teams or groups is different from the more traditional one-to-one supervision format many supervisors and students, especially in the humanities, feel comfortable with and are able to navigate in a secure and professional manner (Handal & Lauvås 2011: 222). With that in mind, the supervisor should be aware of the changed pedagogical conditions for supervision across the different formats applied." (Bengtsen 2014a: 8-9).

The aspect of enculturation, or informal organization, was centrally present in the observed supervision meetings. The space of 'encultured dialogue' (my term) could be seen during the supervisory dialogues when the supervisor and student's voices each found their validity and creativity in thinking on a shared disciplinary platform with joint preconceptions. This was expressed, for example, through discussions of core theoretical works and research challenges. When the supervisor and student discussed these core disciplinary dimensions of the student's research, the dialogue became more dynamic, symmetrical, playful and creative compared to the phases of the supervision meeting when, for example, scientific validity, the academic genre or the demands of the doctoral thesis were discussed. In these latter cases the dialogue and the pedagogical frame became more static, rigid, serious and asymmetrical, and the supervisor and student could be said to argue 'against' each other in a more critical and confrontational manner. So when the supervision meeting addressed themes anchored deeply in core disciplinary concepts and epistemological convictions, the change was marked: the dialogue became freer and more exploratory, even giddy at times. It seemed that in these phases of the supervision meeting the learning potential depended on a playful and creative form of reflection, compared to the more critical and defensive forms of reflection required when the discussion tuned in on validity and genre. Not that the enculturated aspects of the dialogue were 'better' or had any greater learning potential; they were just different, and indicated what can be said to characterize a pedagogy of enculturation.

Enculturation may in this sense be defined as an informal way of organizing doctoral supervision and doctoral education more generally. The disciplinary habit of mind to some extent defines the thinking space of the supervisory dialogue. Depending on the disciplinary paradigm, some concepts and epistemological patterns are more relevant and applicable than others. This was seen multiple times during the observed supervision meetings when the supervisor or student, having been confronted with a challenge to their understanding, immediately sought and found a core disciplinary concept to use as a tool to make space for further analysis. However, it needs to be considered whether these enculturated habits of mind may also, in a less positive way, make the thinking space more narrow than is necessary. To what extent are we as doctoral supervisors kept within our own disciplinary fences, and to what extent does this influence our students in unproductive ways?

In order to maintain the fruitful and creative aspects of the enculturated dialogue and reflection, one could try, as suggested by Dysthe and Samara above, to make explicit and visible the epistemological underpinnings that act as drivers in these part of the supervision. I do not mean to say that enculturated reflection should be formalized, which would probably take the passion and play out of the dialogue, and which would probably also be impossible. Instead, one might try to make the disciplinary preconceptions a conscious part of the supervision to help students understand what the premises are for the core disciplinary dialogue compared to the more general academic and scientific criteria for proper research on the level of the PhD. This is a vital part of the doctoral student growing into a mature academic, who is able at cross-disciplinary conferences and forums to address and discuss scientific agendas and issues with researchers from other disciplines and academic cultures. This is just as much of an issue for the doctoral thesis itself, which is often assessed by a panel consisting of members from different disciplines and academic cultures. The thesis should thus be both deeply anchored in the core disciplinary epistemology and comprehensible to a multi-disciplinary panel. This should help supervisors guide their doctoral students through the core disciplinary issues without having them turn into foggy territory.

2.1.2 Power and emotion

Various studies of how emotions and emotional relations affect the doctoral experience for both supervisors and students (Cotterall 2013; Doloriert, Sambrook & Stewart 2012) have shown that, if acknowledged, emotions can "inspire guide and enhance research (...); if ignored or suppressed, they can delay and even derail it" (Cotterall 2013: 185). The quality of the relationship between supervisor and student is widely recognized as being of crucial importance to doctoral education. As I have dealt with in my previous work, "Lee points out that "poor relationships have been linked to poor completion rates" (Lee 2012: 110), so the aim for the supervisor and student should be to establish a "working alliance, a productive alliance around a shared task" (ibid.). Building on Wisker's earlier work, Lee furthermore writes that "emotional intelligence and flexibility play a large part in working with students through to successful completion" (Lee 2012: 111), defining emotional intelligence as the ability to perceive and express emotions, to understand emotions, to use emotions to facilitate thought and to manage emotion in self and other.

Similar issues about emotions and power are addressed by Manathunga (2014; 2007) and Manathunga and Goozée (2007), who point out the underlying paternalistic setting of doctoral supervision and the supervisor's sometimes contradictory role of disciplinary gatekeeper. Wisker explains the importance of the relationship by noting that "for all students and particularly those working at a distance, the supervisor is the link with the university, and an essential guide, teacher, colleague and mentor in the research process" (Wisker 2012: 81). She also suggests that it is a "political relationship, since you as supervisor have both institutional knowledge and access which can support and inform your work with your student" (ibid.). Arguably, the relationship is even more important for students from different social backgrounds, and for international students, whose social and cultural norms might clash with the supervisor's own expectations of a good professional and personal relationship. As a key factor of good supervision, the issue of the relationship is also fraught with potential aspects of conflict, not only with regard to the interpersonal dimension, but also concerning the quality of the research the student is able to produce. Delamont et al. argue that "precisely because the relationship between a research student and their principal supervisor is so important, disruptions to that relationship are very damaging to the progress, and the quality of the thesis" (Delamont, Atkinson & Parry 2004: 83). Peelo points to the often overlooked connection between the personal and professional levels of the supervisor's role, and states that the "supervision style" of the particular supervisor has great impact on the foundations for building good relationships (Peelo 2011: 28). Across the literature much attention has been devoted to the power relation between supervisor and student. On the basis of work in particular by Barbara Grant, Lee warns about "toxic mentoring" – the destructive side of the power relation in which the supervisor may take advantage of his/her superior position to attain intellectual, commercial or even sexual gain. (Lee 2012: 129)." (Bengtsen 2014a: 13-14).

In Grant's work on power and emotion (Grant 2008; 2005; 2003; 1999), the more troubling sides of doctoral supervision are foregrounded in a consideration of how doctoral supervision can become a "dirty business" (Grant 2001). If the asymmetry and inbuilt hierarchy between supervisor and student becomes too great it can make open dialogue difficult and thus erode the foundation and premise for the act of supervision. Grant succeeds in capturing the power issues at play with her powerful image of doctoral supervision as a "rackety bridge" (Grant 1999). In Grant's words, "negotiating a supervision relation is like walking on a rackety bridge" (Grant 1999: 9). Because of the institutional setting, supervision, like a bridge, gives structure and materiality to the doctoral process. However, as Grant argues, "because of the workings of power, identity and desire, supervision is not static but rackety, a bridge disturbed by erratic movement" (ibid.). The power of Grant's image lies in her point that when "an agreement for supervision is reached, and student and supervisor begin to walk on the bridge together, to act in relation to one another, many unpredictable effects occur, threatening the stability of the bridge and those walking on it" (ibid.). The power structure of supervision exists in its relational dimension, and demands flexibility and openness from both participants in order to maintain the fragile balance of the good supervisor-student relationship.

As I present in my earlier work, "also building on Grant's work, Handal and Lauvås remind us that a supervisor-student relationship consists of "real persons", and, as in all relationships, aspects of gender, social, political and economical status may influence the relation for good or for worse (Handal & Lauvås 2011: 79; see also Lee 2012: 113). Handal and Lauvås, together with Lee, warn of a "too personal" relation between supervisor and student in which the supervisor (or student) may risk being "sucked into the black hole" of the relation, for example when their student's work schedule begins to slide because of "health problems" or "family problems" (Handal & Lauvås 2011: 83). Therefore, as Lee counsels, to maintain a professional balance, personal relationships between supervisor and student must never "become so strong that they are more important than the task" (Lee 2012: 127). Another challenge to the supervisor-student relation is the supervisor's responsibility, during the long process, to keep the student's motivation in balance and maintain momentum in the project (Peelo 2011: 29; Wisker 387ff.). Due to the relatively personal character of the relationship, which may last for years, the boundaries between the personal and professional spheres of the relation may start to become blurred. When facing periods of doubt or strain, doctoral students often turn to their supervisors for help, confronting them with "sloughs of depression about debt, poverty, isolation, thesis problems, and poor employment prospects" (Delamont, Atkinson & Parry 2004: 81; see also Peelo 2011: 27). Some of these issues the supervisor may be able to alleviate, but there are others – particularly problems with the supervisor themselves or their style of supervision – the supervisor may not be able to solve or even recognize.

To ensure that such issues do not overshadow and erode the trust and mutual recognition in the supervisor-student relationship, Peelo suggests that formalizing these elements in advance – and thus making them explicit and open – may ease the dreariness and toil later on in the process. This may be done with "student–supervisor contracts", which can be useful "when the relationship runs into motivational trouble" (Peelo 2011: 29). Addressing a contract formed earlier on in the process, and employing it as a neutral ground for further communication, may help supervisors and students to keep their heads above water and to reestablish a trust that may be threatened or lost. However, as Peelo informs us, "successful negotiation of a period of loss of trust will depend on excellent social and communication skills on both sides, and may well be typified by miscommunication, misunderstanding and frustration on the part of both the supervisor and student" (ibid.). Lee points out that trust and a belief in each other's integrity are central to a healthy relationship between student and supervisor (Lee 2012: 117), and, as it may be difficult to fix broken trust, Wisker suggests that supervisors are mindful of the student's core expectations of an open and friendly supervisor, who is able to balance personal and professional aspects of the relationship in a manner that is empathic and understanding, as well as responsible and professional (see Wisker's list of core issues in Wisker 2012: 85- 87). (Bengtsen 2014a: 14-16).

In the observed supervision meetings the room for negotiation and dialogue played an important and constructive role. However, the power relation was very clear in all of the meetings; the student met the supervisor in order to get feedback and to have his or her work evaluated by an authoritative reader. The individual supervisor acted as the judge of the student's work in a 'trial-like' manner, in which the student sought out the supervisor to receive their verdict on the project. In one meeting, after the supervisor had initially stated that the material the student thad sent for evaluation was OK, the student gave a heavy and audible sigh, claiming that she was greatly relieved and had been very uncertain about her work. During the observations the students were observed to be very dependent on the supervisors' evaluation of their project material; what is more, they seemed to have been kept 'in the dark', without any clear idea about the quality of their work beforehand. The supervisors I observed were all friendly, professional, constructive and helpful in their ways of guiding and supporting the students, but the underlying power structure was inescapable and functioned as a strong organizational element of the supervisory dialogue. That is, the supervisors were the ones directing the agenda, with overall control of the meeting.

Especially during parts of the meetings in which scientific validity and the academic genre were addressed, the supervisors assumed a strong normative voice, using phrases such as "you shall ...", "you should ...", "you ought to ..." and so forth when giving feedback. These normative statements were not meant or expressed in a negative manner, but they show the heaviness and importance of the supervisor's evaluation and judgment, and the passive receptiveness of the students' responses showed their lack of control and power in these parts of the supervision process. Whenever the conversation turned to core disciplinary matters, in contrast, I observed the self-esteem of the students increasing, as they clearly felt confident when operating on the turf of the discipline. This gave the dialogue and dynamic a symmetrical character in which the supervisors' evaluation did not seem to tear so much on the students' energy and strength. In discussions about scientific validity and the academic genre the students' self-esteem was rather low, and they appeared less combatant, weaker and more passive in their engagement in the supervision. Sometimes during these parts of the supervision students spoke up more, but only to defend themselves and fight against the supervisors' feedback, not listening as attentively to what the feedback was about but concerning themselves more with the critical nature of it.

Some of the supervisors commented on this during the interviews, saying that they felt the insecurity of their students and wanted them to take more responsibility for their research project and make it their own. At the same time several of the supervisors underlined the importance of the supervisor's role as the main facilitator with the overall responsibility, if not for the research project, then for the supervision process. This shows how ambivalent and unsettled the supervisors' own understandings of the division of power are during the supervision process. On one hand the supervisors wish the students to take control, and on the other they seem to wish to maintain an asymmetrical underlying power structure. It can be difficult for students to navigate in a relation when the power structure is not overtly addressed or made clear, and when their role, and their power to take ownership over their own project, is not clear either.

During my observations this ambivalence also became visible in another manner. In the supervision meetings the supervisors used the tone of their feedback to influence the emotional space, and thinking space, of the dialogue. In a single meeting supervisors could be critical, inquisitive, curious, serious, playful, humorous, functional and exploratory. The tone was present in how the supervisors asked questions and gave feedback on the students' work. Often these shifts in tone were not explicitly addressed, but worked on a tacit and implicit level. Sometimes the students seemed to intuit shifts in their supervisor's tone, and therefore the conditions for dialogue, and sometimes they were uneasy about what forms of response and options for engagement were possible for them. This revealed the subtlety of supervision pedagogy, but also the complex and, to the students, sometimes confusing polyphony of voices present during meetings.

It should be stressed that in this context power and emotion are not seen as unwanted and unfruitful aspects of doctoral supervision meetings. On the contrary, emotion is highly important for developing and maintaining the students' motivation and momentum during the PhD, and power structures help frame the supervision context in order to give a stable and supportive institutional framework during the sometimes confusing and complex research process. What I want to suggest is that power and emotion, when not overtly addressed and reflected upon by both supervisors and students, can lead to unhelpful experiences of insecurity, self-doubt and anxiety in matters where such emotions could either have been avoided, or even turned into their positive counterparts. The path to using emotions more constructively as a pedagogical tool lies in the way the issue of power is addressed by the institution, by the supervisors and by the students themselves.

A good example of how the articulation of power influences the supervisors and students' understanding of power in specific supervision contexts can be found in Grant. In Grant's work there is a tendency to fuse power with negative words, as for example "dirt" (Grant 2001: 12). On the one hand, the word "dirt" calls attention to the suppressed and often ignored or downplayed challenging conditions the students work in during supervision processes. On the other, it suggests that power and emotion are dangerous and troublesome dimensions of doctoral supervision as such. My point is that power and emotion are neutral aspects of organization, which may have either positive or negative consequences depending on the particularities of each supervision context. As researchers and practitioners we should be able to construct a vocabulary in which power and emotion become visible as pedagogical conditions for every supervision meeting, and not factors already laden with problematic associations. Together with their students, supervisors should introduce a more explorative and transformative discourse about wanted and unwanted power structures in their own supervision practice.

2.2 Non-formal organization

In contrast to formal and informal organization of doctoral supervision and education, 'non-formal organization' designates the blind spots: the parts of the PhD that exist 'below the radar'. Non-formal organization includes things that are not traditionally thought of as constituents of doctoral education, for example private life and private contexts such as 'socializing' within and outside the institution. It also includes the highly personal, or idiosyncratic, aspects of doctoral education that are difficult to contain in formal systems and may be just as difficult to fit into informal communities of practice. Thus, the non-formal parts of doctoral supervision are those that are typically experienced as the most "irritating, (...) imprecise and variable" (Handal & Lauvås 2011: 53, my translation) dimensions of the process. In this section I foreground two central aspects of non-formal organization: firstly the sprawling spaces of doctoral supervision, and secondly the notions of idiosyncrasy, narrative and risk inherent in supervision processes. To conclude, I argue that in contrast to formal and informal organization, non-formal organization is where we should look when we attempt to conceptualize and plan tomorrow's doctoral education programs.

2.2.1 The sprawling spaces of doctoral supervision

The current focus on the parameters of learning contexts for doctoral students questions the primacy of the supervisor's role, as an 'untouchable' position. Contemporary research into doctoral education points out that the kind of support available from the supervisor, or even the institution as a whole, is not enough to guide and support doctoral students in their doctoral journeys, which encompass many other spheres of their lives. As described by Carter (2014) and Carter and Laurs (2014), the role and identity of the researcher change according to what happens in more private spheres of their world, and the energy and focus in the supervision context may be influenced by how the doctoral student is perceived, related to and positioned in relationships outside the university. As McAlpine and McKinnon (2013) state, on a topic that is more broadly addressed by McAlpine and Amundsen (2011) and Nygaard, Courtney and Frick (2011), doctoral supervisors are just one form of support students rely on, and "on a day-to-day basis, students depended as frequently on peers, friends, and family as they did on the supervisors, drawing on each relationship for different kinds of support" (McAlpine & McKinnon 2013: 265). McAlpine and McKinnon show in their empirical study that doctoral students are less dependent on their supervisors when it comes to self-assessment of their progress during the PhD, stating that "supervisors, while important, are not paramount in the doctoral journey" (McAlpine & McKinnon 2013: 278). These findings disturb the dominant discourse in doctoral education that argues for more time at the university and more meetings between supervisor and student. Instead, they call for a more elaborate doctoral pedagogy that sheds light on all the different learning environments the doctoral students participate in, followed by the development of a strategy for doctoral supervisors that enables them to support students in bridging the gaps between these different learning contexts.

In a different study, Jazvac-Martek, Chen and McAlpine (2011) came to a similar conclusion that doctoral students depended on many different formal and informal networks and support systems. They draw on many different resources, and learn in ways that are not easily translated into a generalized academic mindset. Jazvac-Martek, Chen and McAlpine point to "a plenitude of supportive and critical interactions occurring beyond the primary relationship with the supervisor. Students in our research were on the whole well networked and depended on these relationships for different kinds of support" (Jazvac-Martek, Chen & McAlpine 2011: 25). As Elliot, Reid, and Baumfield (2015) point out such 'third spaces', as they call them, could also for the doctoral student include "volunteering in an Oxfam bookshop, going to sports clubs, joining a church choir, or looking after young children." (Elliot et al 2015: 10). As they further describe, for one particular doctoral student, Oscar, "going to the pub opened doors to deeper cultural understanding and social relations with local people, establishing lasting relationships, with one person becoming like a father to him. This, in turn, strongly contributed to a mastery of English – his first major challenge after arriving in Britain." (ibid.). This foregrounds the importance of what happens *between* supervision meetings, and the pedagogical need to articulate these forms of doctoral peer support and peer learning, as well as to negotiate between these contexts and the institutionalized supervision contexts in order to maximize learning potential for the individual doctoral student.

Another thing influencing the PhD and the supervisory context for the student below the institutional radar is what Turunen (2012) calls "snack studies" (Turunen 2012: 72). "Snack studies" are activities that doctoral students pursue when they need time out from their PhD project, to engage more playfully and casually with other academics. This is described by Turunen as follows:

> I took care of my revolt by carrying out 'snack studies'. As the doctoral research appeared every now and then to me as a lonely eternal project, I found it pleasant to do something smaller and together with others. These projects suited me well. However, I guess that my supervisor was not too happy about my starting work with some other research instead of the doctoral one. The snacks were nourishing and opened many opportunities for me both in Finland and internationally. (Turunen 2012: 72)

This points out the often overlooked parts of the PhD in which doctoral students tinker, mess around and experiment with other learning environments and other researchers than the institutionalized supervision context and their assigned supervisors. Another example of this is Zukas and Andersen's (2012) study of how a summer school helped to ease the PhD process in a setting "in which the traditional supervisory relationship and the disciplinary curriculum are deconstructed through intensive group processes" (Zukas & Andersen 2012: 69). The change in scenery determines the way one thinks, speaks and acts, and, as pointed out by Mitchell and Louw (2011), the rhythm and preconceptions, or the "dance", of research driven dialogue. As doctoral students move in and out of all of these formal, informal and non-formal settings it can be challenging both for supervisors and students to align the knowledge and experiences they gain, and the ways they influence the students' further work with the doctoral thesis. Vocabulary and concepts gained from one context can be tacitly transferred by the student to supervision meetings and thus confuse the established norms for the disciplinary language used by supervisor. Not that there is anything wrong with such disturbances – on the contrary they often heighten the level of the research – but it is helpful for both supervisor and student if such transgressions are made visible.

These forms of mergings, overlaps and entanglements of different institutional, departmental, social and personal contexts have been described as "nested contexts" by McAlpine and Norton (2006) and McAlpine and Åkerlind (2010). However, as studies show, we know little about how these contexts are actually linked and nested, or how this structure influences learning and teaching strategies for doctoral students and their supervisors. Sometimes the contexts are nested on the doctoral student's own initiative; sometimes by institutional overlaps not known by the supervisor; and sometimes by means of social environments outside the institutional context. These sometimes aligned and sometimes dislocated learning settings can be difficult for the supervisor to relate to and take into account, meaning that options for differentiation and more individually tailored supervision processes are made difficult or even lost. I argue that we need a more radical image than that of nested contexts for unaligned learning contexts in doctoral supervision settings; I propose the image of a 'sprawl' as an alternative guiding metaphor for doctoral supervision. In this context, 'sprawl' does not denote an uncontrollable chaotic force, but a non-linear and plastic understanding of learning spaces, not limited to formal and informal settings, but including what I call non-formal spaces.

During my observations of supervision meetings it was interesting to see the many different things that emerged and became part of the supervision, but it was often not altogether clear exactly what part they each played. Some of the students planned to participate in conferences and networks without 'asking leave' of their supervisors first. In one of the meetings, the result of this was that the supervisor immediately tried to gain control of the situation by probing the theme and nature of the conference, and persuading the student to align his activity with his overall research focus. The supervisor supported the student in his initiative, but at the same time did not seem comfortable with being left in the dark about his research and collaborative activities. At two other meetings more personal issues were brought up. In the first case, the student was trying to solve practical and financial issues raised by his wanting to bring his wife and children on his research trip abroad. This interfered with his wish to participate in two different international conferences, and he considered cancelling his place at one of them because of the family-related challenges. In the second case, the doctoral student had recently separated from her husband, and was trying to sort out issues regarding their house, children and jobs. This obviously generated practical and organizational challenges for the student, and it was clear that it took a great amount of personal energy and focus as well. In the first case the supervisor acknowledged the student's difficulties and need for support regarding the 'non-formal' aspects of his career, as I have termed them above; he did not, however, feel that it was his responsibility or even in his power to help. In the second case, the supervisor offered personal and moral support to the student and chose to act outside the institutionally defined guidelines for supervisor responsibility.

These situations where different contexts were influencing and even at times disturbing each other during the PhD were handled very differently by the doctoral supervisors I observed and interviewed. Some felt a very distinct need to link these contexts together and create a holistic framework for understanding the doctoral student's work. Others expressed the desire to become familiar with the different contexts that might influence the student's work, though they as supervisors did not feel the need to align them, or see the relevance of doing so. None of the them were indifferent to the non-formal aspects, and they all acknowledged the importance and relevance of keeping such aspects present for the student for him/her to deal with and handle. This all indicates that the interrelated contexts and changing conditions for doctoral work are a highly potent form of organization during supervision meetings and the PhD more broadly speaking. The image of nested contexts is simply not potent enough to contain the degree of dynamism and shifting contexts that condition and influence PhD research. The social, personal and private lives of doctoral students change several times during the PhD, as do their interests, experiences and familiarity with many sorts of disciplinary and cross-disciplinary networks, societies, research groups, coursework and more loosely institutionalized peer collaborations. I suggest the 'sprawl' as a more precise image for the way that non-formal aspects of the doctoral journey organize and impinge on supervision meetings. The sprawl more effectively underpins the sometimes forgotten measures of time, energy and focus non-formal aspects of the PhD demand from the doctoral student, but also their potential for personal development, and newly acquired insights. These non-formal aspects form a very strong organizing force precisely because they often operate in the dark, below the radar.

What are the implications of non-formal organization for future doctoral pedagogy? I find it of positive interest that all the supervisors I observed and interviewed wanted to make non-formal challenges explicit for their students during supervisory dialogues. Some even wanted to support students as far as their skills allowed them in the more personal and social aspects of these issues. However, none suggested that their students should seek help more directly from other members of the staff in the department, and none encouraged their students to seek counsel from other doctoral students or from their family and friends. The supervisors did not seem to understand themselves as a resource that could lead elsewhere, but as an end point – the problem solver himself and not the counselor or guide leading the student to other more qualified sources of support. The supervisors who engaged with the non-formal aspects also tried very hard to come up with solutions to these matters in order to align them with the overall progression and direction of their doctoral student's project.

Based on these findings I want to suggest two complementary, perhaps to some point alternative, approaches for doctoral supervisors in handling non-formal organization in supervision dialogues and students' research frameworks. Firstly, the supervisor herself should draw more openly on other parts of her own professional network, or the networks and professionals of the department or faculty. There may well be other members of staff who have experiences with non-formal aspects of doctoral supervision that could benefit the particular doctoral student in need. Supervisors should also encourage their students to draw more on non-formal forms of support and counsel – to rely on the guidance of peers, friends and family who might be better 'supervisors' when it comes to non-formal aspects of the PhD. In these situations, doctoral supervisors should see themselves more as a means, or a stepping stone, leading the student on to more proficient counselors. I do not mean to downplay the importance of the supervisor, but instead to broaden the view of what supervision, or counseling, during the PhD can be. If we are open to acknowledging different forms of supervision, support and guidance during the PhD, the doctoral student herself will be better empowered to make the most relevant choices for herself and her family.

Secondly, I suggest that supervisors do not force a holistic doctoral pedagogy on their students, urging them to link and align the different parts of their lives with their doctoral program and research agenda. Formal, informal and non-formal parts of the PhD may be difficult to align, and perhaps even when alignment is possible it should be avoided, as they constitute categorically different dimensions of the doctoral journey and the research project. Supervisors should practice their pedagogy in a manner that makes it the student's task to link non-formal aspects of the PhD to their research plan. This does not mean that supervisors should not care or be interested in non-formal organization: rather, it reflects the fact that doctoral pedagogy is not a question of finding a soaring logic for all the different forms of organization encountered during the PhD. Instead, it is about offering the best possible advice to the student, and this sometimes means advising them to seek counsel elsewhere, even if it feels like letting go of the control over the student's project.

2.2.2 Idiosyncrasy, narratives and risk

Non-formal organization does not merely cover the sprawling and mongrel characteristics of the many different, multi-layered pedagogical spaces of doctoral supervision. It also encompasses aspects that are exceedingly difficult to apprehend, as they are almost always caught in a blind angle and nearly impossible to handle on a conscious and reflective level. No matter how much knowledge we accumulate about the generalized roles of doctoral students and supervisors, the individual student will have his or her particular needs, learning strategies and ways of thinking – just as the individual supervisor will have his or her own personal pedagogical style and approach to supervision. I studied such personalized forms of pedagogy in my PhD thesis (Bengtsen 2012; Bengtsen 2011) and used the term 'idiosyncrasy' to identify a new perspective on pedagogy at the university. It is important to stress that such forms of supervisory idiosyncrasy are not a normative derogation of personalized forms of doctoral pedagogy, but an analytical concept that allows these personalized pedagogical rationales and strategies to emerge and become a means for professional critical reflection, instead of living a shadowy existence as 'oppressed' implicit pedagogies. In my PhD thesis I showed that such idiosyncratic aspects are highly valuable, maybe even necessary, to supervisor professionalism and student engagement. These findings links to Gill Turner's (2015) highly interesting use of 'Journey Plots' to illustrate the individual learning journey for new doctoral supervisors. As Turner underlines "the journeys allude to the importance of time to learning to super- vise. By focusing on one supervisory experience from start to finish, rather than a single supervisory incident, the duration and the inter-connectedness of various aspects (e.g. emotions, challenges, agency, resilience) of learning to supervise become apparent." (Turner 2015: 96-97).

In the growing literature on how life-narratives influence and form the doctoral journey and the conditions for doctoral supervision, studies foreground the importance of supervisors tailoring their supervision closely to the individual student, and getting a sense of what Kearns, Gardiner and Marshall (2008: 77) call "the secret life of the PhD student". This so-called "secret life" and its implications for the supervisor–student relationship, and doctoral pedagogy in general, has also been considered in what I call the 'narrative' strand of doctoral supervision research. Such narrative studies have been presented in Bartlett and Mercer (2001a), Määttä (2012), and Engels-Schwarzpaul and Peters (2013) to name a couple of key works. In Määttä (2012) we read powerful PhD experiences as they are recalled by the doctoral students themselves, and as they are understood retrospectively to have influenced their PhD journeys. In Oinas (2012) we are absorbed in a narrative about a doctoral student with 'fox-like' characteristics (here used as a metaphor for shy, but also sly, behavior) who faces many difficulties in her PhD process and who only begins to succeed when she meets a supervisor who knows "how to supervise a fox". In Tulloch (2013) we learn about how fantasy, resistance and passion can become catalysts for the writing process, and how "embodied passion and rage bring my fingers to the keyboard, but paradoxically can also freeze them" (Tulloch 2013: 35). In Bartlett and Mercer (2001b) we see how doctoral supervision practice can be transferred into theoretical frameworks through the use of metaphors based on personal narratives about experiences with doctoral education. Bartlett and Mercer use three metaphors – cooking up a feast, planting a garden and bushwalking – to initiate a conceptual reflection on deeply personal stories about doctoral supervision settings. The concluding point here is that doctoral pedagogy faces new challenges when we bring out into the open the deeply personal and idiosyncratic preconceptions and ways of teaching, learning and thinking that cling to us as supervisors and students. We must develop a more reflective approach to such aspects in our doctoral educational work, since they influence and determine the conditions for how students design their research, and how we support, engage with and scaffold doctoral work as supervisors – often more than we wish to acknowledge.

As I have dealt with in my earlier work, "focusing on different aspects of ambivalence and pedagogical murkiness, Moira Peelo's concept of supervision contributes a singular feature of what I would define as non-formal organization of the pedagogical conditions for doctoral supervision. Giving voice to potential pitfalls and mishaps during the PhD, Peelo points to challenges of unpredictability, which are often downplayed in the handbook literature's functional and directional focus. She describes the phenomenon of "risk" in relation to different aspects of the supervision process. No matter how well the institution facilitates the doctoral program, "teams can go wrong, equipment may not work, and money runs out" (Peelo 2011: 26). While different institutional and administrative systems may be set in place to support and guide the doctoral student during the PhD, "it must be said that the nature of research is to be risky [...]. Had these problems already been solved, then there would be no 'unknown', no level of difficulty with which to engage" (Peelo 2011: 27). Not only can research equipment and time plans work against the doctoral student, but lack of motivation and other personal situations may cause difficulties as well. Students may "begin a project that while once exciting inevitably runs into periods of dreariness and toil. Part-time students may be juggling work and families with research, and often at a distance from the institution" (ibid.).

Peelo combines risk with disciplinary aspects. Risks do not only emerge through economic and practical challenges that demand administrative suave and efficiency – subject matter is also part of what makes a PhD a risky business. From this perspective, risk "is new subject matter, on the edge, taking understanding forward and on sufficient scale to be worthwhile and to be carried out over a long time period" (Peelo 2011: 26). There is no way of knowing where the subject matter will take the student and the supervision process. This aspect of the unknown is foregrounded in Peelo's research, even with regard to the character of doctoral students. Just because the particular student has done well earlier in his or her studies, "there is no real way of telling who is going to manage to succeed and who is not. Intellectual development is not a straightforward process because it has a transformative element" (Peelo 2011: 27). This poses serious challenges for the supervisor, as there is little or almost no way of knowing beforehand if the student is likely to complete or not. Peelo describes how apparent "plodders came through, in the end, with clear and sparkling analyses of interest and originality, while others who started off as high fliers become stolid and stodgy in their conceptualization" (Peelo 2011: 28). As it is notoriously difficult to predict what type of person or learner will have the better chance of coming through in the end, "each supervisor walks into a risky situation each time they agree to take on a student – no promises can be made realistically on either side" (ibid.). It is a risky business for students as well. Supervisors may be excellent in all sorts of ways; they may be personally and socially welcoming and competent, and experts in the given field of knowledge – however, as Peelo states, "their nerve and expertise when things go wrong may not always be the strongest" (ibid.). Supervisors who are experts in the subject, and highly experienced examiners and supervisors, may be "lacking human sensitivity", and they may, "over years of supervising, have lost their excitement and interest in the face of yet another student stumbling through the mists of a PhD" (ibid.). It also happens that supervisors lose patience and prevent students developing their own thesis, as they themselves struggle with time limits and administrative procedures. Supervisors in this situation may insist on a particular shape for the thesis, or a particular style of analysis.

To deal with the challenge of risk in doctoral supervision, Peelo offers advice similar to that described above in the section on formal organization. However, by affording the topic special attention, and by describing its implications at different levels of the PhD journey, Peelo reinforces the notion of risk, making it more potent, more threatening and more real. In the growing literature on doctoral supervision, which often has a functional and problem-solving character, it is important to give heed to powerful counter concepts as well, such as risk, idiosyncrasy and unpredictability." (Bengtsen 2014a: 20-22). This is by and large supported by Brodin's study (Brodin 2014) on creativity in doctoral education and the intimate link between risk and achievement in doctoral research. Brodin quotes Sternberg and Kaufman as she emphasizes that realizing creativity is not possible if the individual is not willing "to take a risk, or to defy conventions, or to fight ideas that others might scoff at" (Brodin 2014: 2). To play with the terms a little, one might question whether non-formal organization of doctoral supervision should instead be termed 'deformal' organization – as such contexts are experienced as twisting and bending the traditional rules and expectations of students' learning and thinking habits. In this way non-formal aspects tacitly shape and form conditions for doctoral supervision. Even if they become present to the supervisor and student as phenomena of 'idiosyncrasy', 'narrative forces' or 'risk', they are still difficult to meet pedagogically. This can be seen from the findings of my empirical study of doctoral supervision meetings.

During my observations of supervision meetings it became clear how pedagogically important the stories doctoral students tell about themselves during the PhD are, as well as how they tell them. Doctoral students have often already formed well-defined researcher identities – identities that may be reformed at different times during their PhDs. At one of the meetings, the doctoral student told a story about himself as particularly critical of some of the prominent researchers in the field. The student was about to participate in a conference where he planned to argue rather aggressively against one of these experts, who was also going to speak at the conference. The supervisor was familiar with the student's narrative about himself, and as he wanted the conference to be a good experience for the student, he tried to be diplomatic and encourage the student to be more nuanced and moderate in his planned criticism. At the same time, the supervisor wished to support the student's independence and critical force and counseled him to stick to his argument, albeit to refine it in order to get more acknowledgement and respect from his opponent.

In another meeting the doctoral student was preoccupied with working through technical and highly theoretical details very thoroughly during the supervision session. The supervisor tried to encourage the student not to hide behind the theories but to be more frank and transparent in her approach. However, at the same time the supervisor clearly sensed that the student was working out her own way through a long and poorly lit tunnel, moving stubbornly and steadily on, an approach the supervisor supported since she was also interested in understanding the topic better. The student was obviously trying to work out something that was deeply important in getting a hold on a key concept in her discipline, and the rigor with which she approached the reflection seemed to astound the supervisor. It was clear at some points that the supervisor was getting impatient, because the progression in the dialogue seemed to hinge on a level of detail that did not seem important to her. At the same time she was cautious not to 'disturb' the student in her methodical journey ever deeper into the heart of the logic of the concept she was exploring. To the supervisor her intense preoccupation with her analysis seemed to make her both strong and independent, and fragile, so that she could not be pushed around too much.

This aspect was also touched upon during the interviews with the supervisors. Many stressed the importance of trying to get 'inside the student's mind' and to learn how the individual student thinks and interprets her own identity as a new researcher. One pointed out the importance of 'locking in' on the individual student's 'ability' – their particular form of independence in academic thinking and learning strategies. The supervisor stated the importance of doing this early on in the supervision process in order to support the student in the most helpful and relevant way. This confirms the view that doctoral pedagogy very much depends on often hazy and shadowy dimensions of the student's personal identity, and the influence these have on how they think about and carry out their research. Independence, in this pedagogical sense, requires the doctoral supervisor to find a balance between the parts of the doctoral student's idiosyncratic and individual thinking and learning strategies that are accessible and tangible – and those that are not.

The non-formal factors of narratives, idiosyncrasy and risk organize the supervision in a way that makes supervisors very aware of them, even when they have no reflective language to describe and understand them pedagogically. These non-formal aspects can be defined by the way they constantly move about on the brink of what is recognizable in a disciplinary sense for the supervisor, and what recedes into the dimmer dimensions of more personalized and individual approaches to doing research and wielding the discipline. This corresponds to Parker's (2005) use of the term "troublesome knowledge" (Parker 2005: 158) to describe the ways students sometimes "clash" with or confront disciplinary codes and norms for talking about specific subject matter. Parker points out that teachers, and in this case doctoral supervisors, must try to align disciplinary and "extra-disciplinary" (ibid.) understandings and accounts in a way that acknowledges the individual student's method of propelling herself into the discipline's core concepts and frameworks while simultaneously maintaining and safeguarding disciplinary norms and habits of mind in order for the student to make herself understandable in a broader disciplinary and cross-disciplinary context. Non-formal organization thus plays a vital part in supervisory dialogues as it ensures student motivation and engagement, and enhances the progressive, dynamic and potent qualities of the student's voice in supervision meetings.

To grasp the organizational powers of non-formal aspects of doctoral supervision and education, we need new ways of conceptualizing doctoral pedagogy. We need concepts that meet the ambivalence and sometimes elusiveness of doctoral supervision practice. As argued in Bengtsen and Nørgård (2014) and Bengtsen and Barnett (2015), the conceptual level of higher education pedagogy must be able to grasp the process-related dimensions of student voice and student work to gain momentum when reflecting on supervisory matters. We need new vocabulary and metaphors for the non-formal aspects of doctoral supervision. In supervision practice, such a focus on types of non-formal organization such as narratives and idiosyncrasy is highly valuable when considering the student's voice. What has become clear to me from my observations and interviews is that personal narratives about researcher identity and idiosyncratic takes on research design are key issues when supporting and enhancing the doctoral student's motivation and engagement with his or her PhD. Therefore phenomena described as 'troublesome knowledge' and 'extra-disciplinary' forms of student work should be taken very seriously by doctoral supervisors: they are the key to finding student enthusiasm and self-efficacy. Risk and risk taking, however difficult it is to manage and to plan for, is of seminal importance to students and supervisors alike. A willingness to take risks can sometimes be an expression of immaturity and naivety on the student's behalf, but often it is the sign of much deeper powers at work that correspond to the ideas which motivated the student to engage in doctoral work in the first place.

2.3 THESIS ORGANIZATION

Presented also in my previos work, "the doctoral student population today has become more heterogeneous, with students from mixed institutional and methodological backgrounds. This has been met with further research into how supervisors can best advise their doctoral students about acquiring the necessary writing skills to fit their research project into the academic genre. Lee describes this as "functional supervision", the meaning of which includes the supervisor's "responsibility for identifying a series of milestones that keep the project on track [...]. The functional supervisor and the student are both clear about the assessment criteria that are going to be applied for examining and the requirements for ethical practices are made explicit" (Lee 2012: 30). These guidelines deal primarily with generic skills across the disciplines: neutrality, objectivity, transparency and the coherence of the PhD thesis as a product to be handed in and assessed. This is to ensure that the thesis is as robust as possible when it is evaluated and assessed by academics who may be from different disciplines.

This form of functional supervision includes both a product and a process dimension (e.g. Handal & Lauvås 2011: 58-59). The product dimension covers advice and strategies for writing up the thesis, such as that presented in Wisker (2012: 415ff.), and Delamont, Atkinson and Parry (2004: 117ff.); in these examples, guidelines are presented for how supervisors may help their students to pose the right research questions, structure the text corpus and divide the thesis into sections and chapters, as well as to manage a larger research project more generally. The product dimension also covers how to prepare for the viva (PhD defense), which questions to expect and how to engage in an open and critical dialogue with the opponents (Lee 2012: 41; Wisker 2012: 471ff.; Eley & Murray 2009: 118ff.). Issues of potential conflict within the review panel evaluating the PhD thesis are discussed in Peelo (2011: 37ff.) and

Morley, Leonard and David (2002), where it is argued that subtle and often tacit rules of conduct and professionalism influence this part of the process: for example, what the supervisor may have in mind when either engaging in dialogue with the panel or suggesting who should sit on the review panel. Finally, the product dimension covers eventual complaints and appeal procedures, which the supervisor might also be aware of in the latter part of the process (Eley & Murray 2009: 136ff.)." (Bengtsen 2014a: 9-10). Grant (2008) also analyses the doctoral thesis as a potential battleground between the supervisor and student. Grant points out that the thesis is the most important 'thing' or artifact as it mediates the negotiations of power and models the dialogues in supervision meetings, as the supervisor "talks *through* the body of the draft to the student" (Grant 2008: 20) when giving feedback on the work.

As I have described elsewhere, "the process dimension covers the challenges of supporting and motivating the student towards completion (Wisker 2012: 413ff.) – what Peelo refers to as facilitating students in "slaying the dragon" (2011: 51). As this phrase suggests, the literature focuses on the student's often challenging and overwhelming task of managing the progress of their research and translating their empirical studies into chapters of a PhD thesis. Dysthe and Samara (2006) and Taylor and Beasley (2010) focus on how supporting students in the writing process also helps them to manage their own research project. Similarly, Eley and Murray give a thorough treatment of the key "feedback mechanisms", the "purpose of feedback" and different "feedback models" that may be applied by supervisors (Eley and Murray 2009: 100ff.). Wisker points out that to ensure completion it is crucial to establish good research processes and practices early on in the process, and to encourage good writing habits and skills (Wisker 2012: 115ff.). Based on the earlier work by Wisker and Delamont et al., Taylor and Beasley pinpoint structural levels of the PhD thesis that the supervisor should ensure the doctoral student bears in mind (Taylor & Beasley 2010: 83ff.), demonstrating that product and process dimensions are always intertwined in the research project. The literature focuses unanimously on the supervisor's responsibility to engage closely with the writing process early on, and to follow the student's working and writing processes throughout the PhD – not to hold the student's hand or do the work for them, but with the aim of helping them manage a project, the format and nature of which will be new to them, and which requires the right tools and skills in order for them to make it their own." (Bengtsen 2014a).

I continue (in Bengtsen 2014a) by foregrounding how Wisker (2012), Wisker and Robinson (2009) and Kiley and Wisker (2009) all place emphasis on what they call "threshold concepts". Wisker wishes to articulate the experiences many doctoral supervisors have of what happens when students approach key disciplinary challenges within their research project that force them to forge new concepts or new interpretations of already paradigmatic concepts within the specific discipline. In the process, Kiley and Wisker draw the focus of doctoral supervision into the disciplinary realm, reinforcing the oft-heard supervisors' claim that supervision is a strange nexus of disciplinary, epistemological and pedagogical axes – a "paradigm" (Kiley & Wisker 2009: 439). Wisker thinks of threshold concepts as the "crucial moments in the research journey, and as ways of identifying when students start to work conceptually, critically and creatively, and so are more able to produce breakthrough thinking" (Wisker 2012: 9). She uses this term to foreground the notion or 'hunch' supervisors may get when they see that the student is about to enter into troublesome, but also potentially illuminating, waters. Threshold concepts should be understood as the research project's "'core concepts' because of the necessary and transformative elements each threshold concept represents. Threshold concepts are discipline or discipline-cluster specific" (Wisker 2012: 13; for more on "core concepts" see Kiley & Wisker 2009: 432).

In comparison with the other works treated in this chapter, Kiley and Wisker give particular importance to disciplinary creativity, "originality and *knowledge creation*" (Kiley & Wisker 2009: 437). Supervising students in their confrontations and dealings with threshold concepts may be challenging, especially because "threshold concepts may represent, or lead to [...] 'troublesome knowledge' – knowledge that is conceptually difficult, counter-intuitive, or 'alien'" (Wisker

2012: 14). The supervisor may find it difficult to help students out of the epistemological quicksand they get stuck in, but when "ideas just do not emerge clearly" and there are "shifts in the way in which a student sees the world and themselves in it", there is a link to the students' "awareness of and confident expression of knowledge creation" (Wisker 2012: 15)." (Bengtsen 2014a: 18-19). This point is reinforced in Starke-Meyerring (2011), where the deep link between the "epistemic nature of writing" (Starke-Meyerring 2011: 80) and identity building is explored, and where it is argued that "writing is transformative in a different sense: it is transformative of writers themselves; that is, it is steeped in questions of identity as identities or subject positions are shaped largely discursively" (ibid.).

I also note earlier that "to help their doctoral students engage with threshold concepts, Wisker suggests that supervisors pay attention to how they work and engage with the students' thinking. They should reflect on whether they are encouraging and empowering students to "work conceptually so that they are being critical, evaluative, and problematizing and creating" (Wisker 2012: 16). This challenge is not about work and research processes, nor finding the way into the academic genre of thesis writing, but helping the student to "become fluent in the discourse of their discipline or interdiscipline" (ibid.). By foregrounding the importance of threshold concepts in doctoral supervision practice, Wisker and Robinson's, and Kiley and Wisker's, work occupies a space between the often assumed cross-disciplinary perspective on generic aspects of doctoral supervision at the university, and a disciplinary-specific perspective that underlines the differences in doctoral pedagogy between particular disciplines. Research into disciplinary-specific doctoral supervision is still rather scarce." (Bengtsen 2014a: 19-20). The overall point of this section, however, is about how the thesis itself organizes and influences doctoral supervision. As has been shown, thesis organization is understood in the literature as the relation between craftsmanship and product. The draft material given to the supervisor before the meeting has an enormous influence on the content and form of the dialogue during the meeting.

In my observations of supervision meetings, the importance and influence of core concepts and thesis structure gradually became clear. The core concepts discussed by supervisors and students were seen as toys and technology at the same time. On the one hand, they were explored as new, and sometimes old, toys – to be played with sometimes casually and distantly, and sometimes wholeheartedly and seriously. In these moments the core concepts attained a plastic character; they were bent, stretched, formed and reformed by the student and supervisor in their dialogue. Furthermore, supervisors in some instances tried to invite or lure students into performing a threshold crossing if they felt they were ready. During some of the interviews supervisors explained how they were scrutinizing their students' ability to actually wield the concepts and not 'merely' use the concepts 'stepmotherly', which in these instances meant 'in a superficial manner'.

At times the core concepts would suddenly stop being toys and transform into a powerful form of technology – tools or instruments to explore the research object in question. In these parts of the supervision meetings, the core concepts were not plastic but rather refined and harnessed to endure the pressure exerted on them by the 'real world' of the context being researched. Instead of playing with the core concepts themselves, the supervisor and student started playing, and even 'digging', *using* the core concepts as a means to another end – to shed light on aspects of the research object. This points to the core concept's transformative nature, as part of a particular form of supervisory 'alchemy' or disciplinary artistry and craftsmanship, since it has clearly defined purposes despite its somewhat plastic character, which is shaped by the dialogue and relation between supervisor and student.

A similar situation was observed regarding the dual role the structure of the thesis was given by both supervisors and students. During the supervision meetings the discussions about the structure of the article, section or chapter addressed could be compared to an act of trying to reconstruct the spine of an animal not yet in existence. Supervisors and students used structure as a modeling tool to form something they did not yet know how to build properly, something that is also pointed out by Cherry (2012). As a pedagogical tool for organization during the dialogues, structure can also be characterized as a kind of navigation tool. But instead of using the structure 'merely' as a map or sextant to steer by, supervisors and students were building the entire ship *while* steering it. In a similar way to the core concepts, the structure of the thesis served a double purpose; while functioning as a way of organizing the argument or analysis at hand, the structure emerged from the very endeavor of structuring itself.

This reveals one of the key challenges for supervisors and students during supervision meetings. Both relied heavily on structure and core concepts during their meetings, and much of the success of the meetings seemed to hinge on the progress made in dealing with them. In the parts of the meetings when the structure did not show itself, and the core concepts did not seem to be of much use in the empirical analysis, supervisors and students appeared to be groping blindly in the dark, in danger of missing the mark or getting lost. This clarifies the ambivalence and double-sided character of the thesis as a form of organization in doctoral supervision. For the supervisors, the core concepts were often tacitly operational as internalized knowledge, and they may have been for many years. To the students these core concepts were more like external tools; often they had only been discovered recently and were therefore unfamiliar. The supervisors had long ago crossed the conceptual thresholds and mastered the core concepts of the discipline, but some of their students had not. To use another image, observing these students was like seeing somebody walking into workshops full of tools, instruments, maps, machines, furnaces, chemicals and so on (that is, core concepts). These tools and instruments are alluring and fascinating to the students, but also confusing and sometimes dangerous to those who do not know how to wield them properly. In the interviews, some of the supervisors wondered why their students did not take more control of the concepts discussed during the meetings. But a workshop full of foreign technology may be intimidating to a person on the other side of the threshold – crossing it is like falling through a rabbit hole. For the supervisor the transition is familiar and safe because she has travelled back and forth many times, but for the student the rabbit hole is fraught with potential dangers and things they do not dare to touch, for fear they might break or explode. On the basis of my observations, it can be argued that supervisors at times overlook how unfamiliar students may be with some of the tools (core concepts) they themselves have held in their hands and used as professionals for years. Not that students are not ready to work deeply with core concepts on the doctoral level – but supervisors must be able to defamiliarize themselves from these concepts in order for them to see the workshop and the world through their students' eyes.

As a central part of doctoral supervision takes place through the use of texts, there lies a pedagogical challenge for supervisors, and also for students to some degree, in externalizing the core concepts and structures of the text in order to put it out in the open, nakedly, so to speak. This demands that supervisors are willing to strip themselves of their conceptual armor and lay down their weapons, or technology, for a while, and to meet the world openly. This calls for open and lucid supervision. I do not argue that supervisors should forget or ignore their own disciplinary mastery of the concepts or methods in use, nor that supervisors should themselves become students again. I argue that to avoid miscommunication and misunderstanding during supervision meetings, it may be helpful for supervisors to step back out of their own workshops, so they can see the conceptual threshold from the other side, and maybe re-cross it *with* the students, in a way that benefits both of them.

2.4 ROLES AND RELATIONS AS ORGANIZERS

How supervisors and students understand each other's roles defines how they relate to each other personally and academically (Lee 2008; Brew & Peseta 2007). As Manathunga points out, the roles we assume as supervisors and students may become good or bad habits, and either way they influence central parameters like learning outcomes and completion (Manathunga 2005b). Depending on what role the supervisor assumes, the student is positioned accordingly. For example if the supervisor assumes the role of the teacher the student becomes a pupil, and if the supervisor assumes the role of the master, the student becomes the apprentice. If the supervisor assumes the role of the counselor, the student becomes the client, and if the supervisor assumes the role of the administrator, the student becomes part of the system that needs to be administrated. Dysthe and Samara (2006) propose that three basic and underlying models for supervision – the apprentice model, the teacher model, and the partnership model – that build on such implicit roles and relations. During a supervision process a supervisor assumes many roles, and even within a single meeting they need to assume different roles according to the tasks that need attention, whether it is "expert coaching", "facilitating", "mentoring", "reflective practice" or "sponsoring" (Pearson & Kayrooz 2004: 104-105).

Roles and relations become forms of organization in doctoral supervision because they are ways of managing, structuring and framing the processes involved. Anne Lee (2012; 2008) shows this in an especially clear and concise way with a holistic integrative framework that includes all the major dimensions of doctoral supervision. This is part of an attempt to give voice to all the different challenges from one overall perspective. Taken from my earlier work is the point that Lee explains that "the framework is about modulating the different aspects of doctoral supervision (Lee 2012: 12), drawing them up, so to speak, through one overall model that can explain the key challenges, acts, solutions and practices of the five categories of "functional supervision", "enculturation", "critical thinking", "emancipation" and "relationship development" (Lee 2012: 5). These categories, or approaches, are "complementary, and the boundaries between them are permeable. They form a useful basis for disaggregating different beliefs and actions in the teaching and the supervisory process" (Lee 2012: 13). The underlying ambition of holism, or a holistic perspective on research supervision, is important for Lee (2012: 1), who argues that it is necessary for good doctoral supervision to take into account disciplinary, pedagogical, humanistic, ethical and political aspects at the same time: the frame is "holistic and integrative, it includes organizational, sociological, philosophical, psychological and emotional dimensions" (Lee 2012: 13).

In defining a unique framework, Lee explains how earlier research projects, using interviews with supervisors and students, built frameworks with key modulators such as the tension between high and low levels of support in relation to high and low levels of structure (Lee 2012: 19), or high and low levels of control in the supervision process in relation to person- versus task-focused approaches (Lee 2012: 20). The point here is not about specific frameworks developed by Lee and others, but the underlying pedagogical concept of doctoral supervision itself as a framework. Lee makes visible how supervisors, and those researching supervision, construct frameworks as they attempt to divide an often extremely complex and multidimensional phenomenon into manageable and transparent pedagogical categories. Lee points out that "one criticism of the framework proposed in this book is that it aims to create too much of a 'tidy reconciliation' of a process which is undeniably messy and individual" (Lee 2012: 13). Integrative frameworks like Lee's can be viewed as too demanding, as they suggest that the roles and responsibilities of the particular supervisor are many and diverse, and not easy to align. However, the potential represented by an integrative framework for doctoral supervision is that it can supply a platform of understanding for supervisors, which initially makes pedagogical reflection easier, or less messy, helping to organize the supervisory task on a mental level and thus giving supervisors specific tools and categories to apply in their own individual practice." (Bengtsen 2014a: 23-24).

As Terry Gatfield (2005) shows in his well known study on supervisory roles and management styles during the PhD, the myriad of structural factors related to PhD completion can be reduced to a basic model, or "supervisory management grid" as Gatfield calls it (Gatfield 2005: 317), which demonstrates a correlation between high/low levels of support and high/low levels of structure (ibid.). Gatfield shows how the different supervisor-student roles and relations change during the PhD, noting how the different phases demand more or less structure and support, captured in the movement between the supervisor types that he terms "pastoral", "laissez-faire", "contractual" and "directional" (Gatfield 2005: 322). Gatfield's point is that some general roles and relations, and "supervisory styles", as he terms them, are used by many different supervisors, and that patterns can be identified according to particular phases of the PhD. Though Gatfield's supervisory management grid is somewhat reductive and limited in scope, it is a helpful tool to make explicit the relation between roles, phases and tasks in one's own supervision practice.

In the observed supervision meetings the supervisors generally directed the conversation. They saw it as their responsibility to ensure progression, and to keep to the meeting's agenda. The supervisors assumed many different roles, acting as teacher, counselor, administrator, colleague and even friend, often all within the same meeting. The students were positioned accordingly as student, client, system, colleague and friend. The roles assumed matched the different issues on the agenda; for example feedback on draft text material; counseling regarding conferences to attend; discussion of relevant courses and how much time and energy they might require; and talking about more private, or practical, issues about how a student might arrange to take his family with him on research and field trips. These roles and relations organized the supervision meeting as underlying discursive frameworks that made it clear what was relevant and what not at any particular point, and when the student should contribute actively to the discussion or listen to the supervisor's feedback. They shaped and organized the meetings differently according to how well the supervisor and student knew each other, and how far along in the research process the individual student was. It also depended on the age of the student and the age of the supervisor, though the gender of the supervisor and student did not seem to be of much relevance in the meetings I observed.

My intention is not to go deeply into the variations or to discuss what roles and relations developed in what circumstances. My aim is firstly to point to the great variation and diversity in roles and relations across supervision meetings, as I have done above, and to draw out the pedagogical consequences. Pedagogically it was observed that the roles and relations assumed and enacted in the supervision meetings to a great extent defined and determined the dialogical space, and hence also the learning and thinking space of the supervisor and student. The roles conditioned how and what questions could be posed, how they might be answered and discussed and also to some degree how much humor or seriousness was appropriate. In many ways the roles and relations became visible as constructive forms of organization and implicit ways of facilitating the supervision meeting. They gave stability, predictability and direction to the meetings, and made it possible for supervisors and students to arrive at a shared footing from which they could more thoroughly delve into discussions of the research project. This is not a new point, but the traditional roles and relations often assumed during supervision meetings have many and diverse pedagogical benefits for both supervisors and students when they engage in a mutual learning dialogue.

However, I also observed the less constructive side of traditional and established roles and relations in supervision meetings. While they established and maintained some learning and teaching opportunities, they excluded others. Like grooves in a record, certain forms of dialogue and even vocabulary and tone seemed to follow from particular roles and relations between supervisors and students. Pedagogical routines that are too powerful or uniform risk hindering new learning opportunities and preventing other ways of exploring the subject matter. In one particular meeting, a young doctoral student was so much in awe of his supervisor that he barely spoke until half an hour into the meeting, and often his comments were merely corrective and elaborative. The supervisor was not domineering, and she kept inviting the student to participate more. In that case, the established roles and relations seemed very powerful and hard to change – even though it was likely neither party wanted them to continue structuring the meeting in such unfruitful ways.

As we know from sociological and anthropological research norms, habits and routines can be very powerful indeed and it can be almost impossible for the individuals that continually reproduce and reenact them every time they meet to change them. However, actions can be taken by supervisors and students to counter unwanted roles and relations and to bring new energy and dynamism into the supervision setting. As Kobayashi, Grout and Rump (2013) suggest, relying on two or even a group of supervisors and co-supervisors can be a way of continuously creating new learning opportunities, giving the doctoral student opportunities to assume new roles and to experiment with the supervisor–student relation and the different reflective dialogues it is possible to have and learn through. Furthermore, peer-learning (Boud & Lee 2005) and the use of research groups and teams and group-based supervision (Dysthe & Samara 2006; Dysthe, Samara & Westrheim 2006; Burnett 1999; Mullen & Tuten 2010) can help to challenge static and circular supervision relationships. As shown by Halse and Malfroy (2010) and Hughes and Tight (2013), the link between feedback practices and thinking and learning practices is strong in doctoral supervision, which points to the central link between epistemological gain and the enactment of different roles and relations in doctoral pedagogy. Experimenting with one's thinking and research potential accordingly requires that one experiment with the roles and relations that condition and influence thinking and research practices in doctoral supervision meetings.

2.5 CONCLUSION

The many different perspectives on doctoral supervision drawn on and discussed in this chapter are traditionally researched and dealt with as separate functioning entities that are either loosely connected or not connected at all to the pedagogy of doctoral supervision. However inspiring and insightful such studies are, they give a somewhat fragmented and confused image of doctoral pedagogy. I do not mean to argue that doctoral pedagogy is a simple and uniform phenomenon, nor that it should be neatly aligned in one holistic perspective. I do not want a new holism in doctoral pedagogy – on the contrary, my point is to give pedagogical value and substance to the doctoral supervision literature by creating a conceptual framework that enables supervisors and heads of doctoral education programs to comprehend the deeply interwoven and entangled nature of doctoral educational practice.

Through a thematic analysis of the literature and discussion of the findings of my empirical research on doctoral supervision, I have shown that what have traditionally been understood as loosely related and occasionally linked features of doctoral education are rather deeply merged and inextricably linked features of a more fundamental pedagogical ore. This pedagogical ore is the educational phenomenon of organization, and I have demonstrated how phenomena as different as supervision contracts, administrative systems, disciplinary cultures, power and emotion, idiosyncrasy and risk, core concepts and thesis structure and roles and relations are all forms of organization that apply in doctoral supervision. They all form, shape, influence and develop teaching and learning opportunities in different ways, and have different consequences for supervisors and students engaged in doctoral supervision practice.

This argument has two key implications. Firstly, it gives supervisors a reflective distance from the different drivers in their supervision practice, enabling them to see the above mentioned aspects as sources of influence that can be arranged differently if necessary. They thus become pedagogical tools instead of predetermined, unquestioned rules. Secondly, and most importantly to my own research, the analysis in this chapter reveals how doctoral supervision revolves around many different axes, since it is organized by many different forms of logic and educational planning at the same time. This shows doctoral supervision as a highly complex, challenging and advanced form of pedagogy, perhaps the most advanced form one encounters in universities. Doctoral education is informed, managed, shaped and transformed by many actors and agendas simultaneously, which makes doctoral supervision unique as a learning and teaching platform, and unique in the pedagogical professionalism it demands from supervisors in universities around the world every day.

PART 3

SUPERVISION AS DIALOGUE

To many doctoral supervisors and students, dialogue seems the only natural choice of communication style for supervision meetings. It allows both parties to explore the student's research perspective and design collaboratively; what is more, it is often referred to as the highest level of interaction in the educational setting, since it demands significant relational and intellectual skills and capacities. But what are the pedagogical and epistemological underpinnings of the supervisory dialogue? What educational values and ideals for thinking and learning are inscribed in the dialogue as a teaching and learning format? And what sets the doctoral supervisory dialogue aside from everyday dialogues and other dialogues in educational settings? Based on the findings of my research project and studies of the literature in the field, I argue that three essential educational features define doctoral supervision as dialogue: (1) teaching format; (2) intrinsic value; and (3) listening and voicing.

3.0 TEACHING FORMAT

Teaching and learning through dialogue is the constituent didactical feature of doctoral supervision meetings. Doctoral supervision can therefore be defined as a 'small group pedagogy' or, perhaps especially in the humanities, a 'dyadic pedagogy' (my terms). In small group pedagogy each participant, all things being equal, has much greater opportunities for engaging in and influencing the conversation than they would in larger groups. This has to do with the nature of the teaching and learning dialogue; on the one hand, it is an educational tool for structuring and managing highly complex conversational patterns, while on the other it is resistant to structure and management. I will treat each aspect of this unique teaching format in the following.

3.0.1 The dialogue as a tool for structure and design

In this section I discuss the structural and directional aspects of the supervisory dialogue. Here dialogue is seen as a relational-didactical structure with which supervisor and student navigate and manage mutually agreed upon educational outcomes. On the structural level, which I deal with here, the supervisory dialogue is often defined as a form of 'dialogism' with reference to Mikhail Bakhtin's theory. As Dysthe, Samara and Westrheim (2006) explain, dialogism contrasts with monologism, where "monologism sees knowledge as a given, dialogism sees knowledge as emerging from the interaction of voices (multivoicedness)" (Dysthe et al 2006: 302). Dialogue is a form of mutual knowledge-building that ultimately springs from tensions and possible divergences of thought, because "where monologism is concerned with transmission of knowledge, dialogism is concerned with the construction and transformation of understanding through the tension [of divergence]" (ibid.). Shields and Edwards (2005) also draw on Bakhtin to define the educational dialogue used in supervision settings. Educational dialogue is described as a knot consisting equally of relational and intellectual dimensions because of its "inextricable connections between dialogism, relationships, and understanding" (Shields & Edwards 2005: 58). Shields and Edwards also point out that in contrast with all other forms of teaching, the educational dialogue demands a unique form of engagement and personal investment (Shields & Edwards 2005: 57). This sets the supervisory dialogue apart as a teaching and learning format that must be understood and reflected upon on its own terms.

For Handal and Lauvås, the relational, communicative and interpersonal dimensions are the main operators and factors by which good supervision is meassured. In my previous work I argue that "they see dialogue as the key 'technology', to be adjusted, applied and formed in different ways throughout the process – as different "forms of supervision" (Handal & Lauvås 2011: 58ff., my translation). In this view, communication is the nerve of successful doctoral supervision, and "efficient communication is dependent on that the people speaking together draw from a sufficient arsenal of shared preconceptions which are at work as tacit conditions for the supervisory dialogue" (Handal & Lauvås 2011: 103, my translation). Importantly, Handal and Lauvås link the dialogue explicitly to disciplinary matters and the depth of research made possible through dialogue. The depth of the supervisory dialogue mirrors the depth of the reflection made available by supervisors capable of facilitating and engaging in explorative and creative dialogues. The dialogue thus becomes the main way to support and challenge doctoral students in their research to attain depth in the subject matter and attain autonomy on the personal-professional level." (Bengtsen 2014a: 22-23). As noted by Li and Seale (2007) in their empirical study of managing criticism in doctoral supervision, the supervisory dialogue, besides being a way of engaging in explorative and creative processes, is also the primary means of giving structured feedback to students. Delivering feedback can be a difficult task and requires what Li and Seale describe as "strategies of foreshadowing, advice-giving, repair, humour and politeness" (Li & Seale 2007: 511). A key point in Li and Seale's study is that doctoral supervision demands, from the supervisor as well as from the student, a highly advanced form of "interactional and communicative skills" (Li & Seale 2007: 522). Such skills are seldom made explicit and trained instrumentally, meaning that supervisory dialogues at the doctoral level are potentially open to an unfruitful degree of randomness and lack of managerial control.

The subtlety and complexity of the communicative and didactical practice inherent in supervisory dialogue is well described by Gina Wisker (2012). She shows how such dialogues cannot be understood univocally, but consist of many different, and sometimes mutually exclusive, pedagogical strategies. Dialogical practice is sometimes used didactically by supervisors to instruct, direct and teach students (Wisker 2012: 196-198), and sometimes to liberate students from the traditional mindset of the discipline and help them create their own personal thinking and learning space by encouraging, supporting, coaching and facilitating learning in more pedagogically indirect and discipline-implicit ways (ibid.). As shown in the influential empirical study by Wisker, Robinson, Trafford, Warnes and Creighton (2003), the supervisory dialogue cannot be reduced to one simple conversational structure, but changes throughout the PhD. The nature of the dialogue in early phases, which often consists in establishing relational trust between supervisor(s) and student and creating a focused and structured research design, is very different from in later phases, when deep thinking and conceptual threshold crossings may be the main driving force. Wisker et al. (2003: 391) list the many different forms of dialogical pedagogy that occur throughout a PhD. In a recent study by Wisker and Robinson (2013) it is also demonstrated that dialogical practice may be influenced by departmental and institutional changes, such as when a doctoral student loses his or her main supervisor and becomes "orphaned". The relational dynamics that such a change often results in can be experienced as a disturbance in the dialogue between supervisor and student.

As Dysthe and Samara (2006) argue, the supervisory dialogue is more than just a dyadic phenomenon; it is also a collective, group pedagogical space. In line with this Janne Malfroy (2005) suggests that the ways we talk and engage in supervisory dialogues very much depend on the expectations inscribed within the particular supervision setting. Research cultures that have strong, shared norms for researching, teaching and learning – a so-called "monoculture" (Malfroy 2005: 175) – may produce uniform conditions for conversational engagement. With an example from her empirical studies Malfroy shows how organizational changes also change dialogic and learning opportunities for doctoral students. In particular, "PhD nights" (Malfroy 2005: 174), or late evening seminars in more relaxed and informal peer groups, have made possible a new, unexpected and highly "powerful pedagogical practice [that] developed the research capacity, of both supervisors and students, and provided a forum for imaginative and intuitive explorations about researching practice" (Malfroy 2005: 177). This leads Malfroy to stress the "importance of collaborative knowledge sharing environments and collective models of supervision" (ibid.), which invite supervisors and students to engage in supervisory dialogue in new and innovative ways.

During my observations of doctoral supervision meetings it became clear to me that it is very hard, as an observer, to separate the relational and dialogical aspects of the supervision meeting. This is the case for all kinds of teaching, as the relational and communicative dimensions are two parts of the same whole. However, in doctoral supervision the relational aspects have more intense and imperative weight *because* the dialogue is the primary teaching and learning format. Seen this way, the dialogue in itself plays a significant organizational role. It is not possible to say that I merely observed different supervisory dialogues across different supervision meetings. Of course this is true to some degree – but I also observed many dialogues during *each* supervision meeting. This chimes with Wisker's point that one dialogue may consist of many different dialogical actions. I draw a more radical conclusion from this than Wisker. Wisker implicitly adopts a holistic view of the supervisory dialogue in which its many different forms are all components of the same overarching dialogue. Conversely, I argue that the many different sub-dialogues cannot easily be framed within one super-dialogue that encompasses the entire meeting. I observed that sub-dialogues could deal with such varied themes as course participation, research design, discussion of theories, health issues and text feedback, and they were not necessarily knitted together during the meeting. I propose that supervision dialogues are in fact more 'shred-like' and 'torn' than the research literature has suggested so far.

During the interviews I asked supervisors and students to what extent they felt that the supervisory dialogue changed character in meetings with new, or other, students and supervisors. The supervisors felt that the conditions for dialogue changed with every new doctoral student, though they did not themselves change their own ways much. The students felt that they themselves changed a great deal depending on the supervisor they were facing – that is, whether it was their main or co- or external supervisor. They implicitly connected the change of relation to the change of dialogue, or the change of dialogue to the change of relation. Some of the students said that the dialogue would change according to how well they knew their supervisor and whether they felt comfortable with them. They described how they entered into supervisory dialogues on the background of trust and familiarity, which means, as pointed out by Handal and Lauvås, that the potential for learning and teaching is heavily dependent on the character of the supervisory dialogue. This aligns well with my earlier research into the relation between personal and disciplinary aspects of the supervisory dialogue at universities (Bengtsen 2012; Bengtsen 2011). However, it also presents a new insight: the personal level influences and conditions learning and teaching strategies in doctoral supervision because it influences the *dialogue*, and not the other way around. This implies that learning and teaching strategies in doctoral supervision grow out of the character of the dialogue, and not the other way around. Dialogue shapes and conditions what learning and teaching can become in supervision settings. The supervisory dialogue thus seems more powerful than individual teacher and student agendas and intentions in themselves.

Wisker (2012: 187) has used the image of choreographed dancing to make this point clear, and Mitchell and Louw (2011) similarly rely on images of dance and rhythm to explicate the interpersonal aspect as prior to the personal, or individual, aspect. In line with this I argue that personality and supervisor and student individuality must be seen in the light of the dialogue's interpersonal core. The traditional division between teacher and learner perspectives in supervision settings should be seen from within the interpersonal relation that the dialogue makes manifest. This focuses on the supervisory dialogue as a central platform for the design and structure of relationship and knowledge building in doctoral supervision. However, in contrast to the formal and informal educational organization of doctoral supervision, this platform first becomes visible in the midst of the dialogue itself as it takes place. Supervisory dialogue is thus revealed as a double-sided educational phenomenon. On the one side the dialogue demands supervisor and student engagement and activity, which provide the dialogue's dynamic flow and progression. On the other, however, the dialogue is also a trace, or result, of deeper underlying relational aspects that are not visible or settled. While it reveals some educational aspects, the supervisory dialogue conceals others. I conclude, firstly, that the supervisory dialogue is not unitary but often plural even within a single supervision meeting, which entails that not one but many pedagogies, or relational drivers for teaching and learning, are present within the same meeting. Secondly, feedback strategies for supervisors and students are highly dependent on the form the supervisory dialogue takes during the meeting – which places even more importance on the dialogue than earlier studies have shown.

3.0.2 The unpredictable dialogue

Supplementary to the aspect of dialogue as structure and design as described above, doctoral supervision dialogues are also defined by their unpredictable and open-ended character. As mentioned earlier on Cherry (2012) describes how the supervisory dialogue is always moving towards a place that does not exist, so to speak, and Handal and Lauvås (2011) stress the fact that no recipe, no map and no fixed endpoint can frame it as it changes its course many times during each meeting. As an essentially relational and dynamic pedagogical phenomenon, the dialogue is in a state of continual emergence, constantly coming into view and into being as it unfolds. Doctoral supervision dialogues are characterized by their loose ends and fog-like (Cherry 2012) qualities. This is seen when the supervisor or student uses the dialogue to question epistemological hierarchies and presumptions, thus opening up new paths and new ways of thinking and understanding the research object.

Shields and Edwards (2005) term this quality dialogical "play and playfulness" (Shields & Edwards 2005: 142), and argue that playfulness in dialogues must be understood in opposition to contained and closed frameworks of thought. When one is totally consistent, "one has stopped being open, stopped learning and growing. Consistency, we might therefore argue, is antithetical to dialogue" (Shields & Edwards 2005: 143). This dialectic quality of the supervisory dialogue has been well researched and described by the Danish educational philosopher Finn Thorbjørn Hansen (2011; 2010; 2008) who argues that openness, and the ability to stand in the open, is the core educational feature of pedagogical dialogues. The openness of dialogues, as addressed by Shields and Edwards and Hansen, does not result in passivity and epistemological paralysis. On the contrary, it is the openness that leads the conversation and the thought on to new discoveries. Shields and Edwards relate this openness to the carnival and the "polyphonic" (Shields & Edwards 2005: 149) thinking space, where new voices and perspectives are welcomed and acknowledged as equally relevant and important as more traditional, hegemonic perspectives on a given subject matter. They point out that the dialogue "mocks the rules of hierarchy and accountability, turning them on their heads, and, in their place, invites others to join the dance" (Shields & Edwards 2005: 150). Empirical studies conducted by Grant (2010) and Bengtsen (2012) support this notion of the dialogue as an entity in itself irreducible to neither the supervisor nor the student. As Bengtsen writes, the "particular supervision meeting can be said to have a life of its own in an autonomous didactical space" (Bengtsen 2012: 9, my translation). Similarly, Grant stresses that the supervisory "conversation takes on its own life even as it is sustained by the participants" (Grant 2010: 274).

As I note earlier on, "this point resounds in Wisker's work, where she describes the supervisory dialogue as a "creative, challenging and empowering dialogue [...], which works rather like a choreographed dance – matching learning behaviours and practices, research project, and learner differences to enable the best outcome" (Wisker 2012: 187). In the "dance", different dialogues are built at different stages in the student's work, enabling the supervisor to get "inside how their question, conceptual framework and methods accumulate" (Wisker 2012: 201); this, in turn, further enables supervisors to work "with them [the students] to plan, reflect, evaluate, achieve and write up their research" (ibid.). For Wisker, the real challenges for supervisors are to avoid taking over (too much), since this can prevent students from owning or understanding their own research, but also to resist withdrawing (too much) from the process, as this can make students feel confused, unclear and lacking in direction (ibid.)." (Bengtsen 2014a: 17).

In line with this, Barbara Grant (2010) writes that supervisory dialogues are primarily about the supervisor and student improvising together, drawing on their former experiences and their deep knowledge about the subject matter in hand. Borrowing imagery from the field of music, Grant emphasizes that mastering the supervisory dialogue is not an easy task as it "requires a kind of flexible, in situ resourcefulness through which players take chances, provoke each other to play beyond their current vision (...), and rework the errors and messes to make musical saves (...) on behalf of fellow players and the music itself" (Grant 2010: 273-274). What happens during this situational knowledge creation and "curricular dueling" (Bengtsen 2012: 145, my translation) does not simply disappear once the conversation ends, because "[s]ometimes what comes out of a save may then become part of the knowledge base" (Grant 2010: 274).

Grant uses the powerful metaphor of "walking on eggshells: breakable and breaking" (Grant 2010: 275) to frame the fragility of supervisory dialogues; as they constantly hover "on the edge of chaos and incoherence (...), improvising dialogues are shadowed by the possibility of collapsing into closure (...) or into an unbearable confusion and anxiety" (ibid.). Being eggshell-like defines the supervision dialogue in all its ambiguity and ambivalence, as the "very fragility of improvisation may also be the condition of its creativity, for uncertainty and risk-taking are central to creative academic work" (ibid.). Engaging in supervisory dialogues demands a relational *and* intellectual sensitivity on the part of both supervisor and student. In many ways the supervisory dialogue in its open and pure form lays bare the supervisor and student's ability to expose themselves as possessing incomplete and imperfect knowledge and a disciplinary reach is limited and to some extent unguarded. Grant summarizes this ambivalence in an inclusive manner that references the elements of conversational dynamism, relational sensitivity and epistemological co-dependence:

> Thinking through the metaphor of improvisation directs our attention towards a vibrant moment in supervision, one in which reciprocity between supervisor and student is a critical feature. This moment is aligned with the kinds of activities that form the creative heart of academic life – the disciplined yet playful sociality of thinking together, exploring ideas, bouncing them off others, following a train of thought, being infected by another's enthusiasms, taking challenges and rising to meet them, coming to ideas you might never have come to alone. (Grant 2010: 284)

This aspect was very clear in the observed doctoral supervision meetings. The supervisory dialogue is the teaching and learning format in which supervisor and student are most strongly dependent on each other because of the core relational aspect inherent in the dialogue as such. Interestingly, this stands in strong contrast to Grant's relational aspects of power and emotion. There may be formal and informal organizational aspects that support the dialogue and anchor it to certain discourses that both supervisor and student may rely upon during their meeting. But the dialogue itself has no such foundation, and it is an experiment every time. This constant presence of the dialogue's potential breakdown is what generates its intensity and focus, which was evident in all the observations. There may be a short or longer interval during the meeting, with the function of a break or pause, but I was never in doubt of when the supervisory dialogue was in operation. The supervisors and students were aware that they were undertaking a form of conversation that would not be successful on its own accord; they needed to do their best to make it work. It is like walking with a full cup of hot coffee without spilling it, or flying a kite, which needs constant attention in order to maintain flow, velocity and height. Like the kite the dialogue is prone to the wind beating at it from all angles at the same time, and everyone knows that the flow cannot last forever, but will be broken at some point when a structural disturbance within the flow itself ends the particular streak of dialogue.

These observations present an important insight that requires further research. Traditionally in doctoral supervision research, the dialogue is acknowledged to have many different functions during one meeting (Wisker et al 2003). Furthermore, as described above, it is understood to be a relational dance and a mutually dependent learning conversation. However, in my observations it became clear that there is no such thing as *a* supervisory dialogue. Supervision dialogues are in doctoral education practice cut up, fragmented, constantly broken and remade, and have, at best, a mosaic-like quality pieced together from many 'dialogue fragments' or shrapnel, which are often scattered around the dialogical space as a whole, but are not necessarily glued together or fitted into one educational frame by either the supervisor or the student. Supervisors and students may start up a thread of dialogue only to abandon it shortly afterwards because one or the other cannot see its relevance, because they are sidetracked by a more pressing issue or because they entangle themselves in subthemes and forget the original theme. One supervision meeting contains several (sub-)dialogues, and these may flare up suddenly with great intensity, insisting on their own importance, only to die out again as the supervisor and/or student lose interest in them.

Another important insight from the observed meetings is the labyrinthine character of the supervisory dialogues. Traditionally, the supervisory dialogue is thought of as possessing a dialectical quality ensuring progress and development and a certain learning output for the doctoral student. But this is not the whole story. In doctoral education practice, dialogues also have a non-linear and chaotic side that leads supervisors and students away from their agreed upon agenda. The supervisory dialogue thus holds within itself a power of seduction and allure that is not easy for students – and sometimes even for supervisors – to acknowledge or control. It was observed many times how the supervisor and student embarked on a dialogical thread about a certain issue only to end up discussing a totally different issue that was not clearly related to the initial topic. Not that this 'snowballing' effect proved to be unfruitful or an annoyance – the point here is that this pedagogical aspect is highly chaotic and seemingly impossible to predict and plan for in concrete supervision practice. Sometimes, though, the supervisor and student did not end up the same place after travelling through the intellectual warp of the dialogue. It is easy to get lost in a dialogue, and difficult to find each other again afterwards. There seemed to be many blind alleys during the supervision meetings that supervisors and students could end up in, meaning they had to backtrack to find a shared footing again.

To characterize this aspect of educational dialogue I have elsewhere (Bengtsen 2013) used an image of a great system of bridges going in all sorts of directions at the same time, moving both towards each other and away from each other at the same time. This has been done to frame the supervisory dialogue as a 'multi-directional phenomenon', which has a plastic and molten core that constantly shapes and reshapes itself according to the situation. In Deleuze's vocabulary, it can be argued that the supervisory dialogue "endlessly produces folds" (Deleuze 2006: 3). The many sub-dialogues of each particular supervision meeting are folded together and seem to create further folds of sub-sub-dialogues even as they are occurring. Following Deleuze, I could dramatically strengthen the point that each supervisory dialogue is not a single linear, dialectical progression, but "[d]ividing endlessly, [and] the parts of matter form little vortices in a maelstrom, and in these are found even more vortices, even smaller, and even more are spinning in the concave intervals of the whirls that touch one another" (Deleuze 2006: 5). Similarly, drawing on Alphonso Lingis (1996; 1998), it can be stated that a dialogue is not "a framework, an order, or an arrangement, but a nexus of levels" and such levels "are not dimensions we can survey from above; we find them not by moving toward them but by moving with them" (Lingis 1996: 33). When engaged in supervisory dialogues supervisors and students seem to have the "sense of abruptly dropping from one wave of duration to another" (Lingis 1998: 69), and these 'dialogical-levels' (my term) pull us in: they "emerge (...) as directives that summon, by following them a field unfolds" (Lingis 1998: 37).

Besides being a pedagogical tool for supervisors and students to give structure and direction to supervision meetings, and the research process in general, the supervisory dialogue is also 'tool-defiant' and unpredictable. This is not to say that its unpredictability is any less intrinsically helpful than its instrumentality; both condition the teaching and learning experience on their own premises, for good or for worse. Unpredictability, however, demands a particular form of presence and pedagogical awareness from the doctoral supervisor. Flying a kite demands a strong force in order to counter the flux and pull from the kite. It also demands great skill, experience and knowledge of wind conditions and aerodynamics, as well as an intuition about when the next pull will come and what effects it will have. Unlike the instrumental and directional quality of the supervisory dialogue described above, this unpredictable quality means that the supervisor has to focus on *re*-acting, becoming more a facilitator and less a teacher. Mastering the supervisory dialogue necessitates an acknowledgement, from supervisors as well as from students, that it takes two to fly *that* kite.

3.1 INTRINSIC VALUE

Even though underlying power relations and 'darker' regulatory forces may be present in supervisory dialogues, Handal and Lauvås still claim that the ideal is the power-free, mutually engaged dialogue found, for example, in the philosophy of Jürgen Habermas (Handal & Lauvås 2011: 106). This Kantian-inspired perception of the goal of doctoral education as the development of personal and professional autonomy is so deeply rooted that we have great difficulty in perceiving it otherwise. The Enlightenment heritage of autonomy is typically fused with early and mid 20th-century philosophy and psychology of intersubjectivity and dialogue, notably found in Martin Buber (2013), Gabriel Marcel (1952), Carl Rogers (2003; 2004) and Emmanuel Lévinas (2000; 2003), and forms the foundation for our preconceptions about the underlying ethics of doctoral supervision dialogues.

3.1.1 Ethics, emancipation and growth

As stated by Shields and Edwards (2005), a prerequisite for being able to engage in dialogue at all is "the ability to intellectually and emotionally sense the emotions, feelings, and reactions that another person is experiencing and to effectively *communicate that understanding* to the individual" (Shields & Edwards 2005: 102). To be able to supervise, as such, you must be able to care for the student(s) you are supervising. However:

> [c]are is not a soft, fuzzy, and nebulous quality antithetical to rigorous intellectual inquiry; indeed care is not anti-intellectual, but a pedagogical approach that takes into consideration the interests, aspirations, and aptitudes of the learner. Thus, it is care that permits us to respond "differentially" to our students. (Shields & Edwards 2005: 102-103)

Following Buber and Carl Rogers, Lien (2011) defines the essence of the dialogue as "contact", and the ability to come into contact with the person you are supervising (Lien 2011: 46). This does not mean, however, that the supervisory dialogue as a phenomenon of mutual satisfaction and learning is a relation between two similar and 'equal' subjects. Rather, it builds on the premise that supervisor and student learn from each other's 'otherness' (Lévinas 2003, see also McPherson 2011); neither supervisor nor student can, or should, assimilate each other's horizons of meaning into their own, but should respect the other person's independence and otherness as a fruitful and enriching feature of doctoral supervision. According to this perspective, being a good supervisor "hinges on making appropriate distinctions between I-it and I-Thou relations, between treating people as subjects (small s) and Subjects (capital S), or between treating people as objects or as human beings worthy of absolute regard" (Shields & Edwards 2005: 108). Underlying, and superseding, the educational relation between supervisor and student in which the supervisor is acknowledged as superior in knowledge and skill, is the ethical relation between two persons in which each person is equally worthy of respect and esteem.

Halse and Bansel (2012) discuss the ethics of what they call the 'learning alliance' (Halse & Bansel 2012: 385ff.) between supervisor and student in doctoral supervision. They stress that for excellent PhD research to happen it is crucial that the supervision practice is well anchored in a constructive ethical framework. This should be an ethics in which the doctoral student is not treated as "a generalized Other" (Halse & Bansel 2012: 385), but is responded to as a "specific, individual 'I' or 'Thou'" (ibid.). Building on Joan Tronto's four principles in care ethics, it is suggested that the supervisory dialogue should base itself on principles such as:

> i) attentiveness that actively seeks awareness of others and their point of view; ii) responsiveness that motivates individuals to extend oneself on behalf of others; iii) competence to do something about the needs of others; and iv) responsibility involving taking care of and assuming responsibility for care. (ibid.)

As Alma Whitely (2012) points out, ethical ideals and virtues are not only a central part of the supervisory dialogue, but also "[permeate] supervisory conversations concerning qualitative research" (Whitely 2012: 260). She goes on to state that ethics and ethical criteria are 'doubled' (my term) as they may simultaneously permeate the pedagogical layer of the supervisory dialogue *and* the content of the dialogue, in, for example. discussions about research ethics. This dimension of caring and responsibility also extends into the organizational layer. As noted by Wisker and Robinson (2012), doctoral students sometimes get trapped or caught in the institutional system, for example if they lose or dissolve the contract with their supervisor – thus becoming 'orphaned'. However technically coherent and organizationally robust the institutional set-up and support systems may be, the system itself cannot take on the kind of pedagogical responsibility only human beings can perform. Wisker and Robinson emphasize that doctoral supervision "interlocks personal (ontology and personal issues) and intellectual (epistemology, conceptual threshold crossings) dimensions from the start, linking learning, personal/professional, and institutional dimensions" (Wisker & Robinson 2012: 151). This finding of their empirical studies shows that, when reflecting on the ethics of the supervisory dialogue, it is necessary to take into account aspects of the organizational structure that merge with, even if only tacitly, the interpersonal and often dyadic learning and teaching dialogue.

If we look into the handbook literature on doctoral supervision, which deals more closely with prescriptive teaching and learning guidelines for doctoral supervision than the journal literature, we find that it agrees on the importance of supervisors supporting and facilitating doctoral students' development of what is referred to as "emancipation", "rational autonomy", "personal development" (Lee 2012: 94-95), "autonomy", and "growth" (Wisker 2012: 108, 191). As I write in my previous work, "enabling emancipation on the students' behalf is achieved, for Lee, when "students find their own direction and values and [...] decide to apply them to their research" (Lee 2012: 94). Furthermore, Lee stresses that emancipation has a very different objective from enculturation. The academic "who is working within an emancipatory framework will not be seeking to keep their students within the discipline, whereas this will be the prime objective for the academic who is working within the enculturation framework" (ibid.). Wisker links autonomy to the level of originality of research expected from a doctoral student (Wisker 2012: 189), and, in line with Lee, links autonomy not to personal growth as such, but to the student's research (ibid.). According to Wisker, this poses a challenge for the supervisor in balancing and navigating in the tension "between hands-on support and the hands-off encouragement of autonomy, and autonomy which will enable the graduate or postdoc to conduct their own research projects" (Wisker 2012: 189-190). Delamont, Atkinson and Parry (2004: 34) state that this dilemma has been visible in empirical studies of doctoral supervision as far back as the early 1990s, and that it constitutes one of the most crucial challenges for doctoral supervisors. Delamont et al. stress that most supervisors experience "a pull between their desire to exercise tight control and to allow the student the freedom that comes from non- interventionist supervision" (ibid.). This point strikes at the heart of a key issue in doctoral supervision pedagogy. Lee points out that it can easily lead to the "dark side" (Lee 2012: 106) of supervision, in which the untrained supervisor does not facilitate the autonomous growth of the doctoral student's research project, but instead makes the student work in line with their own agendas of self-promotion. It can also be difficult to define exactly what autonomous research is, and what personal-professional autonomy looks like. As Wisker writes, this can vary a great deal between educational levels, culturally, contextually (disciplinarily) and individually (Wisker 2012: 188). The supervisor should therefore bear in mind that the student's work matches the level of the degree undertaken, where "greater autonomy and originality are required over a greater length of time for a longer, more significant project, making a contribution to knowledge, and justifying the award of a doctorate" (Wisker 2012: 189).

In contrast to the challenges supervisors meet when supervising students' writing skills and academic craftsmanship, as described above, the literature points to a modal shift when it comes to promoting and enabling emancipation and autonomy. To meet this challenge, the supervisor must switch from being a teacher to being a facilitator. Drawing on Carl Roger's theory of facilitation, which is highly influential in the understanding of supervisory dialogue, especially in Scandinavia, Lee states that "facilitative interventions are those where the practitioner is seeking to enable the student to become more autonomous" (Lee 2012: 102). Drawing also on work by Heron, Lee identifies a hierarchy of facilitator states that the supervisor can use to navigate in the process (ibid.). Reviewing these states, it becomes clear that as the supervisor becomes more experienced and skilled, a higher degree of empathy is successfully manifested towards the student, together with an ability to recognize what may be best for them. This differs from coaching, in which the student, or client – who is autonomous in a different way – makes the decisions. Facilitation is still a form of supervision as the supervisor endeavors to assist the student in developing their research according to the student's own visions and goals, while remaining aligned with the requirements and criteria for good academic research at PhD level." (Bengtsen 2014a: 11-13).

3.1.2 Caring for the research!

In the interviews, supervisors and students alike emphasized the attainment of scholarly autonomy as one of the primary learning goals for doctoral students; this corresponds well with the findings of earlier studies. Disciplinary autonomy and scholarly and personal emancipation are considered to be at the heart of the doctoral experience. However, during my observations of supervision meetings it became clear that although different supervisors articulated their understandings of autonomy in a very similar manner during the interviews, their methods of promoting and facilitating student autonomy were very different and difficult to compare. Even though all the supervisors had foregrounded the importance of autonomy in one way or another during the interviews, in the meetings some supervisors were directive and didactical while others were less overt in taking the initiative, letting the student become the main driver of the supervisory dialogue. These differences in supervisor roles were reflected in the corresponding roles of their students. As such, this supports the notion of supervisor and student roles as plastic and transformative teaching and learning platforms that change over time, across different disciplines, departments and personalities, which is found in Gatfield (2005), Lee (2012; 2008) and Gurr (2001).

Another interesting finding points to the fact that autonomy and emancipation is as much an intellectual (maybe even epistemological) issue as it is an ethical (and relational) one. In the interviews, more of the supervisors linked student autonomy to the fact that "it is *their* project", meaning that the students should ultimately show that they are able to take ownership of their research project and thesis production. This was reflected in the interviews with the students, where they frequently stressed that autonomy is the ability to conceive original ideas and form creative research designs on their own with only a little guidance from their supervisors. For supervisors and students alike, autonomy in the PhD is linked to the formation of *ideas* and *research designs*, and the personal, or existential, aspects of autonomy often described in the literature are mentioned, if at all, in little more than a 'supporting role'. In this light, taking ownership of one's PhD means taking ownership of the growth and formation of *ideas* relevant to the discipline, as well as planning, organizing and conducting research in an innovative and creative way. On the basis of this finding I argue that autonomy and emancipation in doctoral supervision should be understood as an *epistemological* (intellectual-disciplinary) issue – rather than, or at least as much as, an ethical (relational) one. Or, to put it differently, that the ethics, and relational dimension, of doctoral education should deal not only with persons but also with ideas and research designs – which means that taking care of and responsibility for good doctoral supervision means protecting, nurturing and enabling the growth of *thought*.

Another finding shows that while the understanding and role of autonomy may seem clear during interviews with supervisors and students, it is less obvious when observing supervision meetings. This points to a schism between the sometimes idealized understandings of autonomy presented in interviews, and the 'real' and more 'messy' character of actual supervision meetings. Observed supervisory dialogues are neither linear and formative in an obvious way, nor are they beautifully composed pieces of ideal pedagogy; on the contrary, they are fragmented, spontaneous, vulnerable and chaotic. During the observations it became clear to me that autonomy may also be said to include the student's ability to put faith – almost a blind trust – in their supervisor's ability to foresee difficulties and to guide them and keep them clear of troubled waters.

Furthermore, the observations also seemed to show that autonomy requires students to lower their guards and to weather rather hard blows to their project from time to time. This suggests the importance of good judgment to autonomy: It is about when to trust (and distrust), and *being able* to trust (and distrust), one's supervisor(s), as well as having the capacity to differentiate between your project and your person when receiving criticism. As early as the 1990s Acker, Hill and Black (1994) highlighted the complex and deeply personal character of supervisory dialogues, writing "[t]he tendency for supervisors to report adaptations and changes suggests that it is incorrect to view supervisors as having a particular supervisory style independent of circumstances" (Acker et al 1994: 491). Similar themes have been taken up in the literature since, for example in research into the messy and power infused nature of doctoral supervision meetings by Grant (2005; 2008) and Manathunga (2007; 2014), and in Bengtsen's (2011; 2012) studies on the influence of idiosyncrasy in supervision pedagogy. On the basis of the findings of my observations, I challenge the understanding of autonomy as intrinsic to supervisory dialogues. Autonomy can with equal right be said to be constructed, or deconstructed, as a consequence of the wider context of the supervisory dialogue, and it can also be said to relate to the research more than to the student as a person. I suggest that future research into the relational and ethical dimensions of doctoral supervision reconsider the scope of ethics, and whether it is perhaps more relevant to address it in relation to the intellectual-epistemological rather than the personal-relational dimension of supervisory dialogue.

Besides the newfound intellectual-epistemological dimension of the ethics of doctoral supervision dialogues, Halse and Bansel (2012) reveal an equally central cultural dimension. They argue that doctoral supervision dialogues are often understood within the "person-centered paradigm [that] has its origin in the late 1980s and places the personal attributes, roles, behavioral styles and subject formation of the supervisor and/or student as central to the work of doctoral supervision" (Halse & Bansel 2012: 379-380). According to Halse and Bansel this paradigm is not in itself wrong, but it does have limits regarding the way the dialogue is framed and conceptualized. Their conclusion is as follows:

> Whilst the person-centered paradigm has provided insights into the characteristics and approaches of supervisors and the experiences of doctoral students, its usefulness as a conceptual or policy framework for doctoral supervision is more limited. Lists and categories of supervisor attributes, roles and styles are invariably idiosyncratic, oversimplify the complexity of supervision, and sidestep the fact that a supervisor takes up multiple roles in any single interaction with a student and that a supervisor's roles and practices change throughout the student's candidature. (Halse & Bansel 2012: 380)

Indeed it can be difficult to know to what extent the dialogue between the individual supervisor and student is more or less powerful and has more or less impact on the research process – or whether their dialogue, as argued for example in Gardner and Mendoza (2010), are more forcefully influenced by departmental organization, workplace atmosphere and the tacit disciplinary norms and traditions more generally. In my interviews with the students in particular it was stressed several times that workplace and departmental norms and routines for how supervisors interact with and relate to their students have great significance for the character of the supervisory dialogue. The students felt that the tone of the conversations with their supervisors when receiving feedback on their work is to some extent framed by 'cultural' norms and values inherent, not in the dialogue itself, but in the sociocultural discursive norms and habits underpinning the dyadic or small-group supervisory dialogues within a particular discipline or department.

During the observed supervision meetings the different points made by supervisors and students often referred to other dialogues with other people in other contexts- for example, at conferences, during PhD courses or in other research groups. This finding discloses the pluralistic character of supervisory dialogues, and the fact that the particular supervisor-student dialogue is merely a small part in a sea of feedback dialogues occurring in different parts of the academic arena. From this perspective it can be argued that it is not necessarily the supervisor–student dialogue that ensures growth and emancipation during the PhD. Rather, the dyadic supervisor–student relation knits together other dialogues, bridging dialogues between different actors and environments within the larger organization. Although this seems to mean more feedback systems and forms of dialogue become available to the individual doctoral student, it can also be more difficult to settle discussions about who has responsibility for their work.

Acknowledging the complexity of the dialogue and the different personal, disciplinary, departmental and institutional stepping stones that each in different ways potentially help the doctoral student to develop an autonomous and emancipated research expertise, it is also important for supervisors to know where, or with whom, the student can anchor his or her research and personal investments in a deep and trustful way. A handful of the supervisors interviewed stressed how important it was that students have someone to go to when hard times set in. The supervisor may not be the main person that the student seeks out for personal support, but when it comes to disciplinary and research based issues they could be engaged with good reason. Both the interviews and the observations supported this point about the necessity of the student having someone to act as the main facilitator of their personal development. The student cannot be expected to keep everything together herself, at least not initially, but should be assisted by others, whether by the supervisor or a group of supervisors and fellow doctoral students. Though it does not seem to matter whether it is always the same people, or key go-to persons within the institution, that ensure the dialogue is built upon a pedagogical dimension of intrinsic value, intrinsic value itself nevertheless seems vital for ensuring autonomy and emancipation during the PhD.

3.2 LISTENING AND VOICING

Listening is widely recognized to be an essential part of counseling and guidance in clinical as well as educational practices. In clinical practice, the doctor's ability to listen is linked to their power to heal patients (Shipley 2010). As Shipley clarifies the defining attributes of successful listening are "empathy, silence, attention to both verbal and nonverbal communication, and the ability to be nonjudgmental and accepting" (Shipley 2010: 125), and in addition "listening is a deliberate act that requires a conscious commitment from the listener" (ibid.). Drawing on Carl Roger's work on listening in clinical therapeutic contexts, Dana Levitt (2001) points out that in a counseling situation, listening has a twofold meaning and purpose. Firstly, listening in a deep and profound manner enables clients to trust the counselor, and secondly it enables the counselor to influence the client in a positive and constructive way (Levitt 2001: 102). In the following two sections I focus first on the meaning and relevance of active and deep listening in doctoral supervision, and second on the notion of student voice in supervisory dialogues.

3.2.1 Active and deep listening

In doctoral supervision both supervisor and student are often said to be engaged in 'active listening'. Also drawing on Roger's work, Denise Batchelor (2008) defines active listening in contrast to passive listening. Passive listening carries connotations of "spongeous absorption of what the speaker communicates, a porous listener somehow impervious to and unchanged by what s/he hears. The activity and energy are all on the speaker's side" (Batchelor 2008: 49). As Batchelor notes, "[a]ctive listening is not about activism" (ibid.); it does not mean that the supervisor kidnaps the dialogue and takes over the student's project, because such activism would imply a lack of interest and/or competence in listening to the student and understanding things from their point of view. This foregrounds the tricky and advanced form of *teaching* that active listening represents. It is arguably the defining and essential feature of doctoral supervision and what sets it apart from all other teaching formats. Active listening designates the supervisor's double maneuvers of teaching and learning at the same time. The view of active listening as a form of learning activity on the supervisor's behalf is also referred to as "deep listening" (Brearley & Hamm 2013: 259). To listen in a deep way means "taking the time to develop relationships and to listen respectfully and responsibly. It involves reframing how we learn, how we come to know and what we value as knowledge" (ibid.). Batchelor thinks of this double maneuver as a special form of restraint found in supervisory dialogues:

> The active element in listening paradoxically entails the exercise of restraint. This amounts to far more than passive waiting. It involves an inner activity by the listener that is the opposite of directive activism targeted at the student. It requires the listener's readiness to hold back, to be silent, and to develop the capacity to be open to new possibilities of meaning in what s/he hears, to be prepared to be surprised and changed. The listener's openness then in turn frees the speaker to use the silence to explore *his/her* own current meaning structure. (...) Listening actively to the student experience in order to understand it entails listening to what its constituent elements mean to the speaker, not what they might mean to the listener if s/he were in the student's place, or are intended to mean by the institution to a generic student. The active listener is probing beneath the words used to the unique meanings with which the speaker has invested those words.
> (Batchelor 2008: 49-50)

A recent study of active listening in doctoral supervision by a Danish research team (Godskesen & Wichmann-Hansen 2013) shows how important it is that new doctoral supervisors are trained in active listening, because this is an important element of relationship building and student-centered communication. Godskesen and Wichmann-Hansen argue that active listening is especially central to doctoral supervision because of the teaching and learning space it creates between supervisors and students for mutual exploration of ideas and research design opportunities (Godskesen & Wichmann-Hansen 2013: 145). In line with Batchelor, they stress that the key goal of active listening is to enable the supervisor to 'lodge' her perspective within the mind of the doctoral student and to think *from* and *with* the student perspective during their dialogue – not in order to control or dominate but out of recognition and respect for the student's own research perspective and learning approach.

Yet again with reference to Rogers, Godskesen and Wichmann-Hansen write that it demands a good deal of self-efficacy on the supervisor's part and "a great deal of inner security and courage to be able to risk one's self in understanding another" (Rogers quoted in: Godskesen & Wichmann-Hansen 2013: 148) and to "risk coming to see the world as he [the doctoral student] sees it. We are threatened when we give up even momentarily, what we believe and start thinking in someone else's terms" (ibid.). The principal argument of Godskesen and Wichmann-Hansen's study agrees with Batchelor's work on active listening: The good doctoral supervisor should aim to use the supervisory dialogue not (only) to teach, but to *learn with* the doctoral student. This helps us define doctoral supervision as a mutual learning enterprise and a pact of mutual exploration between supervisor and student.

During my observations of supervision meetings it became clear that supervisor listening is performed in many different ways. Some of the supervisors needed to talk quite a lot in order to listen actively; they were using their own words to probe the student's ideas and encourage them to speak out. In my opinion it would be incorrect to read this 'talking-listening', or 'loud-listening', as a way of avoiding listening to the student and so as to force the supervisor's will upon the project. On the contrary, I observed that this group of supervisors used their own words and thoughts as tools and instruments that they offered to the students in their joint exploration of the subject matter in hand. This was especially the case in meetings where the student was a bit hesitant or too nervous to offer up his own ideas straight away. This supports the idea that active listening was being used by some of the supervisors as a strategy for luring the student into participating more in the dialogue. In meetings where this succeeded, the supervisors then toned down their own participation in the dialogue and became more neutral and moderate in their engagement.

In contrast to the above, some of the supervisors were almost totally silent for long periods of time, allowing the students to talk themselves 'out in the open'; the supervisors thus acquired a better view of the thoughtscape of the research project. This was more typical of supervision meetings in which the student was a more active participant within the dialogue. Supervisors who adopted this form of active listening intended, by being silent, to see further into the students' research perspectives and to absorb the students' own vocabulary, key terms and ideas, as well as the structure of the particular part of the thesis discussed during the meeting. In this mode of listening the supervisors would typically emerge from their self-imposed 'silence exile' by degrees, finishing with a longer period of feedback and comments.

The aspect of listening was used by supervisors and students alike as a search mechanism or 'dialogical radar'. Even though both supervisors and students generally seemed very well prepared for the meetings, at times they still needed to locate or re-locate each other's horizon of understanding of the particular subject matter in hand. The character of the issues being addressed was often so complex that on several occasions during one meeting they had to resurface from the technical and highly discipline-specific matter and reassure themselves that they were on the same page. These constant shifts between listening for the other's perspective and voicing their own gave the dialogue a fragmented and staccato-like character at times, as the act of listening was cut up, or disturbed, like a bubble that is burst as it is being blown.

Finally, the doctoral supervisors and students were typically listening attentively *for* something. In the literature on active listening in supervisory dialogues, it is considered to be a way of facilitating teaching and learning opportunities. However, my observations point to an often overlooked didactical aspect of listening – the content, or the 'what', supervisors and students listen *for*. Whether it was a particular form of argument or an idea, a trace of insight in the student's phrasing, an inherent flaw or potential in the underlying research design or a quirky (and thus potentially original) finding in the empirical data, the supervisors were listening for something in particular. This does not mean that listening *to* the doctoral student, and thereby recognizing his autonomy, was neither observed nor overtly intended in the listening – because it most certainly was, as described above. However, the fact that supervisors also listen for 'something' in the dialogue is often erroneously downplayed in the literature on doctoral supervision.

The fact that doctoral supervisors listen, actively, for something in particular – as opposed to whatever the student wishes to say – is what most significantly sets active listening in doctoral supervision apart from active listening in clinical and therapeutic contexts. Doctoral supervisors and students listen actively for highly specific and deeply disciplinary content. Consequently, active listening in doctoral supervision is actually *not* about the person being supervised, as it would be in clinical and therapeutic contexts; it is less about the person and more about the content. This means that our understanding of active listening in doctoral supervision should move from the focus on its role in relationship building to its association with creative and critical thinking.

Once more, my findings point to the idea that dialogue in doctoral supervision is as much a way of *thinking* as it is a way of communicating and relating to others. The need for a renewed focus on 'thought' and 'thinking' in doctoral education, and higher education pedagogy more broadly, resonates both in Gibbs and Barnett (2014) and in my own previous work on supervision in higher education (Bengtsen 2011; 2012). It is also supported by earlier findings in Whiteley's work on 'rigour' as part of the thinking that occurs in doctoral supervision dialogues (Whiteley 2012). Whiteley stresses that doctoral supervision dialogues are a way of testing and evaluating the rigour of the individual student's argument, data collection and research methods, in which "the doctoral student is also an instrument of data collection" (Whiteley 2012: 255). This blending of 'speaking' and 'thinking' in supervisory dialogues has also been addressed in Grant's work (2010), where she describes the supervisory dialogue as "an interplay between her [the supervisor's] thinking and the student's" (Grant 2010: 277). When dialogical 'listening' is being rewritten as 'thinking', thought processes become something that we actively listen for and engage in. In this light, listening actively to the doctoral student means 'teleporting', or projecting, one's thoughts into the student's thought perspective – and vice versa. 'Thought teleportation' (my term) is a process in which the supervisor's and student's thoughts 'jump', or 'leap', from one horizon to another – shuttling between a shared and collaborative ground to the deeply personal and hidden thought complex of the individual person. This is what Batchelor (2008) describes as demanding a great deal of energy and skill on the supervisor's behalf, as it requires a strong and eager will *to learn* from the doctoral student, as well as skill and interest in seeing the potential of the student's research despite its potential irrelevance to the supervisor's own work. Students themselves are aware of this; in the interviews, many of them stated that it is easy to detect and see through a supervisor who "is pretending to be interested" in the student's research project, but who lacks sincere engagement and motivation.

To listen as a form of thinking, and to think as a form of listening, thus demands that the supervisor co-craft the dialogue and thoughtscape with the student, and that both put serious effort into thinking and listening to each other in a deep intellectual-epistemological way – but this also means that they can enjoy, together, the satisfaction of having overcome challenges in the research process together. The placing of *thought* as an inherent feature of active listening in doctoral supervision sheds light on a technological and mechanical notion of supervisor listening. The pedagogy of active listening in doctoral supervision includes a strong operation of *thought*, and the ability to be co-crafting the doctoral student's 'research engine': the deep disciplinary mechanics at work. To listen actively the doctoral supervisor's thought *operates* with that of her students.

Active listening in doctoral supervision is a highly advanced skill that is difficult to master and challenging to teach to new supervisors. Because of its advanced relational *and* intellectual nature, it also relies on the supervisor's authenticity and personal presence, which includes empathy, emotional maturity and a nonjudgmental attitude – as well as a disciplinary knowledge that helps them to follow the student's thoughts, empirical studies and arguments. These findings push the idea of active listening in doctoral supervision into a new and dimly lit space, which needs further research.

3.2.2 Student voice

Giving voice to one's research project is the student equivalent of the supervisor's active listening discussed above. Whereas listening, in the literature, is supervisor-oriented because of the teaching perspective, voicing, in the literature, is student-oriented because of the learning perspective. However, while listening is typically connoted with positive and constructive forms of pedagogical and disciplinary abilities and responsibilities, voicing often has a more ambivalent and undefined character. Denise Batchelor is well known for her pivotal research on the nature of student voice in higher education settings (Batchelor 2006; 2008; 2014), and she argues that the meaning of "[f]inding a voice could refer not only to a student developing an individual voice of his/her own, but also to students developing a collaborative voice whether pedagogically, in relation to their university, or in relation to the broader higher education system or wider society" (Batchelor 2014: 157). In the end, having a voice is primarily about the individual student's (in this case the doctoral student's) capacity for learning:

> Having and expressing a voice are to do with creativity and self-expression, the profession of self and the injection of what one is into the outside world. (...) Losing one's voice is partly about lacking some or all of the capacities for creativity, interpretation, self-profession and self-projection. (Batchelor 2008: 41)

For Barnett, too, the possession and development of student voice is central to enhanced learning in doctoral supervision settings. What the supervisor listens for is precisely this particular student voice, however fragile and premature it may be. It is the power and the formation of the student's voice that ultimately determines whether or not their disciplinary contribution becomes powerful as well. Student voice is central in supervision settings, where the student is "pressed for *her* stories, *her* reasoning" and through her educational voice "is realizing herself and inserting her into her [educational] offerings" (Barnett 2007: 93-95). In doctoral supervision settings giving voice to the student's research project is not an individual but a collaborative enterprise. As Barnett and Coate point out, it is when the supervisor and student are carrying out the 'voicework' through a collaborative effort that a "*togetherness* quality of a curriculum" (Barnett & Coate 2006: 141) becomes possible. Batchelor also describes what she terms "reciprocal voice" (Batchelor 2008: 44). By voicing their project and research endeavor together with their supervisor, the student attains the resilience and courage to develop his own voice more forcefully.

However, finding one's own voice as a doctoral student is not easy; it is often fraught with uncertainty, doubt and worry. Ray Land (2008) emphasizes that developing new and original academic knowledge can often result in "'alien' or 'troublesome knowledge'" (Land 2008: 134) that takes a lot of effort to mold and transform into a valued academic voice. During the PhD such experiences may cause what Barnett calls "ontological discomfort" (Barnett 2007: 76), where the doctoral student loses faith in himself and starts to doubt not only the quality of his research progress, but also himself as a person, which may eventually lead to prolonged periods of stress or anxiety and even the student abandoning his doctoral studies. According to Batchelor doctoral supervisors should be aware of these darker sides of student voice, which point back to the core pedagogical and ethical challenges described above. However, she also writes that this is a primary condition of developing a strong and resilient student voice, which can be especially difficult if the organizational framework housing the particular doctoral student does not leave much room for such moments of crisis:

A contemplative voice is exploratory, uncertain, not always in control, and suffers periods of obscurity in thought that may seem like failure. It can be an apparently unproductive voice without an immediate clear result, whereas the student voice today is required to be demonstrably productive rather than speculative, matured and developed rather than matur*ing* and develop*ing*. (Batchelor 2008: 54, my italics)

As noted by the contemporary American philosopher Alphonso Lingis (2007), voice is not interesting because it tells me about *me* as such, but because it tells me about the fabric of the world (the research object) that we are studying. Importantly Lingis explains that "[a]n empirical science is not simply an additive accumulation of observation reports; it is an exploratory system" (Lingis 2007: 27). This is relevant in supervision settings when supervisors and students give voice to the project by talking through the research material or core theoretical concepts – which corresponds to the threshold concepts mentioned by Kiley and Wisker (2009) and Grant's argument that doctoral supervision dialogues take place through the thesis (Grant 2008).

These points are supported by another contemporary American philosopher, Graham Harman (2005), who uses the terms "charm" (Harman 2005: 134) and "allure" (Harman 2005: 141) to describe the way we are captivated by particular phenomena that give *us* a voice, and not the other way around. Harman writes that we are most happy when we are caught up in our projects, and when we become absorbed by the strangeness and peculiarities of the subject matter we study. He states that "[f]reedom itself is never an absolute good, and is often a troubling void filled with addiction, hopelessness, confusion, or fantasies of triumph and revenge" (Harman 2005: 141), continuing "[c]ontrary to the usual view, what we really want is to be *objects* (...) distinct forces to be reckoned with" (Harman 2005: 140). I use this last point to argue that supervisiors and student do not necessarily wish to survey the entire thesis from above, but want to become absorbed within it, to *be part of it*.

Applied to the context of doctoral education, this helps us shed light on the phenomenon of student voice in a different and untraditional way. Following Lingis and Harman, the voice of the doctoral student does not develop and mature from within the doctoral student as a *person*, but from within the research as an force in itself. This creates different connotations for student voice and for voicing one's research project as a doctoral student. It foregrounds the interplay between supervisor(s), student(s) and research (or thesis) in a way that is not often seen in studies of supervisory dialogues. With Harman's concept of 'allure', the conditions for the supervisory dialogue are changed. Instead of the traditional view in which doctoral supervisors pedagogically aim at promoting good learners and autonomous researchers, the focus shifts to how supervisors and students together listen to, but also become entangled with (or maybe even trapped in), the research design and research process as a force in itself. This, once more, shifts the focus here from interpersonal ethical and relational offerings and actions to an interplay of a more intellectual-epistemological nature based on thought, speculation, data entanglement and the forging of new core concepts to move the discipline forward.

In the interviews many of the supervisors were occupied by the idea of listening and "tuning in" to the individual student's learning and thinking approach. They explained that the aim of this was to help develop the student's voice to allow them to produce a strong and original research project that would be a significant contribution within the discipline. The students also said it was essential that their supervisors could help them find and develop their own voices, with which they could find their own ways into the wildernesses of the discipline. Both supervisors and students focused almost exclusively on the development of the students' voices, and although more of the supervisors expressed hopes and even expectations that the students would surpass them during the three-year long PhD in obtaining a specialized knowledge of their research object, neither the students nor the supervisors themselves expected that the supervisor's voice would be disturbed or changed much. The voice-work was thus understood to be student-focused, with the supervisors playing a guiding and assisting role.

In contrast to these expressed opinions, as well as the descriptions of the ideal form of supervisor listening found in the literature, my observations show that supervisors do not listen 'deeply' to the student's perspective. This discrepancy may be explained either because listening from within the student perspective is too difficult for many supervisors, or because it is actually of less relevance than in clinical counseling and therapeutic contexts. What did happen during the supervision meetings was that the supervisors seemed to be 'voicing' just as much as the students, and that the students seemed to be 'listening' just as much as the supervisors. In many of the meetings the supervisors and students seemed to be on much the same footing most of the time when they were 'voicing' the individual student's research project in a shared exploratory thought-space. When the supervisors and students were listening, they did not necessarily seem to listen for the other *person's* perspective, but for the resonance or echo from the research project itself, which was made manifest through dialogue and voicing. This does not mean that supervisors are not doing their job properly, but instead that the concepts and vocabulary they use to talk about listening do not quite match the pedagogy they actually perform in their supervision practice. It also reveals that the pedagogies supervisors perform are arguably more advanced than, or at least different from, the language and concepts available in the research and handbook literature on the subject. Listening is clearly important for supervisors, but it is a kind of listening that we do not quite comprehend as outsiders, and that they are not necessarily skilled at articulating themselves. It is a listening that projects itself into a disciplinary space that people outside the discipline have a very hard time grasping pedagogically, and supervisors have difficulties in 'translating' it into a general academic language.

Again, a person-knowledge schism seems to emerge from the empirical observations. The phenomena of listening and voicing were, in the interviews with the supervisors and students, tinged with a dualistic language, as if there were persons (the doctoral supervisor and student) behind, or maybe even beyond, the research project breathing life into its otherwise lifeless body. My observations of the supervisory dialogues, on the other hand, showed that there was no such 'distance' between the student or supervisor voice and the subject matter discussed during the meeting. In the interviews, supervisors and students used vocabulary that drew on a form of doctoral pedagogy that separates the person from the research project. This may of course be necessary in many contexts, especially when discussing matters of a more practical, administrative or institutional nature. However, when addressing the core disciplinary issues of the students' research projects, such a distance did not seem to exist. On the basis of this finding I argue, with Barnett (2015), that we need to focus more on "epistemological rhythms" (Barnett 2015: 125) and less on discursive patterns and typologies for personalities or learning and teaching styles during doctoral supervision meetings.

Instead of continuing our analyses of communicative patterns when discussing active listening in doctoral pedagogy, we should instead, as Barnett suggests, conduct a "'rhythmanalysis', (...) an analysis of rhythms embedded in different fields of knowledge" (ibid.). Elsewhere, I have made a similar point about how the current understanding of dialogue in doctoral pedagogy has a tendency to focus more on persons than on knowledge. My findings call for a renewed focus on the knowledge dialogues in supervision meetings, and on the "deep epistemological nerve going through the entire phenomenon of doctoral pedagogy [which is] often overlooked or ignored" (Bengtsen 2014b). To further understand the ways listening and voicing emerge as phenomena in doctoral supervision meetings, we need to move from a 'dualistic' pedagogy in which the person of the researcher 'transcends' the research project, to what can be termed a 'monistic pedagogy' – which, though not holistic, sees the person of the researcher and the research project itself as immanent in the same act of supervisor or student voicing.

3.4 CONCLUDING REMARKS

The main argument in this chapter is that the supervisory dialogue in doctoral supervision practice is a singular and distinct relational-ethical and intellectual-epistemological phenomenon that is nevertheless difficult to conceptualize. As has been shown, the supervisory dialogue contains many seemingly paradoxical features and challenges, which during analysis discloses many intriguing potentials for teaching and learning strategies. The different features that are uncloaked should not be understood as excluding each other, because they are not reducible to each other; rather, they are expressions of different but interwoven relational and intellectual demands and imperatives, which may even complement each other in strange and unpredictable ways. Another key conclusion is that there are some words and concepts found in the research literature and also used by supervisors and students themselves in interviews which arguably confuse and blur the 'actual' supervision practice observed. I argue that it is high time that doctoral supervision discovers its own vocabulary and conceptual framework for dialogue, instead of adopting frameworks from clinical and therapeutic practices that are not entirely suited for the job. This is not to say that the dialogues in doctoral education are more important or difficult to master than professional teaching and learning dialogues elsewhere, but that dialogues in doctoral supervision have their own characteristics that are impossible to reduce to, or assimilate into, those of other professional practices. The three major findings of this chapter are presented below, followed by a discussion of some of their implications for a future understanding of the doctoral supervision dialogue.

Folds more than progressive conversation
Contrary to holistic descriptions and understandings of the supervisory dialogue as one fluid and dynamic conversational and thinking space, I argue that they are fragmented and multidimensional in

nature, containing many pedagogical spaces and vectors that operate in each other's blind angles. This point was illustrated by demonstrating how the supervisory dialogues were simultaneously didactical and controllable, unpredictable and chaotic and singular and plural. The point was reinforced with Deleuze's concept of the "fold" and Lingis' concept of levels. The supervisor and student collaboratively produce various levels and folds in thought and knowledge, performing these folds in the supervisory dialogue itself.

Valuing knowledge more than persons
In research on value and ethics in doctoral supervision contexts, the focus is traditionally set on the personal growth of the doctoral student and their supervisor-facilitated learning, leading to maturation, emancipation and autonomy. However, my study disclosed that during supervision meetings supervisors and students alike are primarily focused on the maturation of ideas and thoughts, the autonomy of the research project and protection of and caring for the core ideas of the project. This suggests that a person-centered paradigm of doctoral supervision dialogues should be supplemented by a *thought-centered paradigm*, which supervisors and students themselves enact and perform, and which seems to encompass the fundamental meaning of value in doctoral supervision practice.

Voicing thoughts more than listening to persons
My observations of supervision meetings showed that doctoral supervisors and students do not listen so much to and for each other as for the 'epistemological nerve' of the subject matter explored in the specific research project. When doctoral supervisors and students listen, they are also, and to an equal degree, voicing – speaking into a shared disciplinary and personal-epistemological thoughtscape. They do not so much listen for each other's voices as for the echoes and resonances of their epistemological voicings. The question arises whether this voicing is a specific form of listening that we do not yet know much about, and if so whether future research should pay more attention to empirical studies of doctoral supervisors' particular and strange form of talking-listening or thought-listening.

The findings in the present chapter by no means set aside or abandon the more traditional knowledge about humanistic ethical and formational ideals of autonomy and emancipation in doctoral supervision dialogues. In doctoral supervision, supervisors and students surely enter into an interpersonal dimension, but more importantly they (also) enter into an 'inter-epistemological' dimension – where the virtues and values of growth, maturation, autonomy and emancipation are first and foremost understood in relation to the individual student's *research* perspective, *research* idea and *research* design. Their focus is essentially on the potential contribution of knowledge, which is first and foremost of an intellectual nature. This discloses an ambivalent concept of doctoral education in which person and knowledge are not always valued equally, pointing to challenges in doctoral pedagogy about how to frame, design and facilitate supervision that has this two-sided focus and goal.

These findings give rise to a renewed discussion about generic pedagogical and didactical skills and approaches within doctoral education, as they show a strong tie between pedagogy and knowledge-work that is not easy to parse. I argue that we need to readdress how we perceive, conceptualize and teach the pedagogy of the supervisory dialogue. I also argue that supervisory dialogues in doctoral education are less a person-centered phenomenon as a knowledge-centered one, which destabilizes the traditional psychological and therapeutic underpinnings of the concept of dialogue in doctoral supervision. Instead I have pointed out the close relation between doctoral pedagogy and epistemology, and even theory of science, which should be more closely investigated and incorporated into the developmental work within doctoral supervision practice.

PART 4

ADVANCED PEDAGOGY

Building on points made about the organizational and dialogical variation, complexity and diversity in doctoral supervision settings in the two previous chapters, this chapter presents and discusses five emerging core structural constituents of what can be called an advanced doctoral pedagogy. Based on my interpretations of the research literature and empirical findings presented in the previous chapters, a new conceptual framework for doctoral pedagogy can be developed – a framework for an advanced pedagogy. This pedagogical framework for doctoral supervision consists of five elements that will be treated separately here. These five elements present doctoral supervision as (1) an ambivalent pedagogy, (2) a subtle pedagogy, (3) an idiosyncratic pedagogy, (4) an embedded pedagogy and (5) a torn pedagogy. This discloses doctoral supervision as constituting an autonomous pedagogy of its own, which should be further researched and developed, as well as taken into account as such by the supervisors, students, administrators and directors involved in doctoral education.

4.0 AMBIVALENT PEDAGOGY

Building on my findings in chapters two and three I formulate here the first definition of doctoral supervision as an advanced pedagogy. It is argued that 'ambivalence' is at the heart of doctoral pedagogy. In this context, ambivalence does not connote flawed, failed or dysfunctional supervision processes, but represents a necessary condition for the entire theatrics of role making and relationship building so important to doctoral pedagogy and doctoral supervision processes.

4.0.1 Role-theatrics at the heart of doctoral pedagogy

Since the earliest studies into the nature and challenges of doctoral supervision, the focus on supervisor and student roles has been fundamental. These roles have been linked to what I call 'ambivalence'. Ambivalence should not in this context be understood negatively, but as signaling one of the essential and generic pedagogical parameters of doctoral pedagogy – that supervisor and student roles may change over time, according to context, personal circumstances, research culture and department etc. That the very conditions for supervision, and therefore also the learning and teaching opportunities, change and vary during the PhD process has been a point of interest since Jennifer Welsh's studies on research supervision in the late 1970s and early 1980s (Welsh 1978; Welsh 1981; Welsh 1982) and the pioneering work done by Ernest Rudd in the UK (Rudd 1968; Rudd 1975; Rudd 1985) and Katz and Hartnett in the USA (Katz & Hartnett 1976). Welsh points out that "great variety" (Welsh 1978: 82) quickly becomes visible when the understanding of roles is seen from a person-oriented perspective. Similar findings lead Bowen and Rudenstein (1992) to conclude that "from all evidence available, [doctoral supervision] is perhaps the most variable of all variables, because it depends so much upon individual personalities, styles, and expectations" (Bowen & Rudenstein 1992: 260). This point has been echoed in the exact same wording in studies undertaken both in the 1990s (Acker, Hill & Black 1994: 496), and in more recent times (McAlpine & McKinnon 2013: 267). Almost 30 years before Gatfield's (2005) study of the dynamism of doctoral supervisor and student roles and styles and Lee's (2008; 2012) well-known framework for doctoral supervision, Welsh (1978) formulated the ambivalence inherent in doctoral pedagogy:

> As a supervisor, the staff member's role changes. He is no longer the unquestioned authority on the subject his student is researching. His knowledge of the student's research area may not be extensive, his proven research ability limited. He finds himself in a situation in which he no longer has complete control. It is for him as much of a learning situation as it is for his students. His authority may be threatened, his expertise as an instructor challenged. His position is no longer that of master but rather of fellow learner. The qualities he requires successfully to fulfill this role are very different from those he requires to be an effective teacher. The staff member may thus find himself in a situation of role conflict resulting from having to attempt to reconcile the incomparability between the two roles he plays simultaneously. (Welsh 1978: 84)

This statement emphasizes the role conflict the doctoral supervisor may experience, and the implications this has for decisions about what form of pedagogical approach to assume and how to apply it in practice. The role of the doctoral student, modeled on the ideal of the 'independent researcher', poses equally challenging potential role conflicts about how to understand the relatively 'simple' matter of ownership of the PhD. This is also described early on by Bargar and Duncan (1982):

> In the practical world of Ph.D. scholarship it seems a gross oversimplification to propose that the Ph.D. student take *sole* responsibility for her own research. In reality the student works under a mentor (sometimes of her own choice, sometimes not), meets the expectations of a reading committee, and conforms to the standards of the graduate school. Typically the student is in continuing interaction with some small community of scho-

lars including her graduate student peers. And perhaps most important for our discussion here is the deep concern the major advisor often has for the substantive nature of the research problem, the methods employed to solve it, and the quality of the research effort as a whole. Whose scholarly reputation is on the line during the final, oral defense? (Bargar & Duncan 1982: 21-22)

This discussion continues in the literature through the 1980s (Rudd 1985; Brown & Atkins 1988) and 1990s (Leder 1995; Hockey 1996; Grant 1999), right up to the more recent studies presented in chapter two, section 2.5. It is interesting to see how the understanding of supervisor and student roles during the 1970s and 1980s is attached to persons and personalities, and how they cope with role changes during the supervision process in comparison with their other tasks as supervisors and students. This perspective alters during the late 1990s with, among others, Hockey's (1997) study on the 'craft' of doctoral supervision in which he moves away from focusing primarily on doctoral supervisors and students as persons to the pedagogical abilities, powers and skills of the supervisor – the supervisor's craft. Among other important pedagogical abilities and activities, one of the central aspects of this craft consists in "balancing" the "complex and composite role" (Hockey 1997: 48) of the supervisor that "harbours a number of responsibilities" (ibid.). There is an inherent tension, or ambivalence, in the difficult but nevertheless deeply essential challenge for the supervisor to "balance the degree of control they exercised over the direction and development of their students' research" (Hockey 1997: 50), which at the same time should "[allow] students sufficient freedom to develop intellectually, and to produce innovative and original research which would gain them the award of a doctorate" (ibid.). Finding this balance in doctoral supervision is especially challenging because it demands the supervisor switch between different pedagogies and different ways of relating to the doctoral student.

Different researchers have interpreted this balance between pedagogical roles and actions in different ways. Wisker and her research team (Wisker et al 2003) describe the many different and subtle nuances of the supervisor role observed during meetings and reveal the deep link between supervisor roles and the implied pedagogy that follows from them. This point is taken up in a study by Mainhard and his research team in Holland (Mainhard et al 2009), which shows the diversity and subtlety of supervisor and student profiles when engaged in doctoral supervision. Gatfield (2005) shows how such role complexity attains new forms over time, noting the inherently dynamic nature of the role positioning aspect of doctoral supervision. Lee (2008; 2012) is probably one of the best examples among recent endeavors to link doctoral pedagogy and roles; unlike earlier researchers such as Welsh, who saw doctoral pedagogy from a roles and relations perspective, Lee focuses on actions and work strategies.

I argue that this change in the view of roles between the 1970s and today should *not* be seen as a movement from a lesser to a greater understanding of the link between roles and relations, or to a more professional focus on doctoral pedagogy. On the contrary, these different studies unlock different, but equally important, dimensions of the meaning of roles and relations in this context. They also show us that roles and relations should not be seen either as a personal *or* a professional feature, but both. Part of the essence of doctoral pedagogy consists in this double act, or pedagogical parallel, of always at the same time assuming a relational form, through roles, and a professional approach or strategy. Seen across the different studies on the meaning and implications of roles and relations in doctoral pedagogy conducted over the last 40 years, it becomes clear that doctoral supervision demands that supervisors and students play out, or live out, a series of fundamentally different learning and teaching perspectives. One of the essential constituents of doctoral supervision is 'role-theatrics', and the ultimately impossible task of balancing conflicting, and comparing incomparable, mutually exclusive pedagogies and mindsets. This, I claim, is the ambivalence essential to doctoral pedagogy, which sets it apart from any other pedagogy in higher education.

4.0.2 Role-theatrics with a twist

To show more specifically what I mean by the inherent ambivalence that constitutes the advanced form of doctoral pedagogy, I will describe how the individual supervision meetings I observed could be said to consist of several pedagogical micro-cosmoi revolving around two fundamental pedagogical challenges. I argue that the diversity of student and supervisor roles in doctoral supervision are to a certain extent determined by one core ambivalence shared between two essentially different pedagogies. This means that instead of seeing doctoral supervision as a mosaic of role pedagogies, as already hinted at by Brown and Atkins (1988), or constituting a complex framework for supervision as more recently proposed by Anne Lee (2008; 2012), my contribution is to put forth the essential, and rather simple, condition of ambivalence as constitutive of a central part of doctoral supervision in general. I do not wish to create a totalitarian or unnecessarily deterministic view of doctoral supervision, and I do not argue that the core ambivalence found in my own study is the only one, or that I have thus exhausted the whole role-discourse within doctoral supervision research. My aim is to view the discussion of roles in a new light and to give reasons for why roles seem to be a general aspect of doctoral pedagogy.

As shown in the schema below (Figure 1), I have followed Handal and Lauvås' (2011: 58-59) simple but powerful distinction between process and product supervision (also referred to in chapter one, section 1.5). However, to accentuate my own point, I have called these two forms of supervision 'supervising *with* the individual student' (process supervision), and 'supervising *against* the individual student' (product supervision). When supervising *with* students, supervisors assume a position from which they 'lodge' themselves as much as possible within the student's own mindset and endeavur to see the arguments, findings, research strategies and potential crises in the project from the student's own perspective, creating a 'student-double', or a 'student-twin' – though they are not of course a real student, but a 'supervisor-student'. This form of supervision is more specifically described in the section on 'Listening and voicing' in chapter three, section 3.2. Supervising *against* students does not in this context mean that supervisors try to sabotage their students' project ideas and research plans, or in any other way intentionally undermine the students or force them from their chosen track. The term covers the positions that the observed supervisors assume when they view the students' work from an external perspective – an assessment perspective, the perspective of the disciplinary community or the perspective of an expert within the relevant field of research. This form of supervision is more specifically described in the section on supervision as a teaching format in chapter three, section 3.0. I am not arguing that supervising *with* students is a better or truer supervision strategy than supervising *against* students. My point is an analytical one: Both supervision pedagogies are equally important because of the different potential opportunities they create. In the schema below I have illustrated the very different, but equally important and central, 'fibers' that constitute the core pedagogical actions observed across the different supervision meetings. I have listed how these two mutually exclusive and unaligned core actions could be observed in relation to:

- Purpose: The basic intention of the pedagogical performance
- Role (relations): The types of role and forms of relation constituted
- Atmosphere: The mood and tone of the dialogical performance
- Style of thinking: The implicit structure of the argumentation taking place
- Language: The speech acts inherent in the chosen linguistic style

The observed purpose of supervising *with* their students was to engage in an explorative and collaborative effort with the students. The joint endeavor was to learn and to investigate the research topic creatively. The observed purpose of supervising *against* students was to evaluate critically the character of the students' ideas, findings or research designs – or to give text feedback on their draft material. From a role perspective, the relation between doctoral supervisor and student is symmetrical and dialogical when supervising *with* students, as the hierarchy is momentarily abandoned with the intention of creating a space for equality between supervisor and student. When supervising *against* students, an asymmetrical relation is immediately established, giving privilege to the supervisor voice and often resulting in supervisor monologues and student passivity.

When supervisors supervise *with* their students the atmosphere is often humorous and playful; together, they create a learning alliance and support each other in the exploration of subject matter at hand. When supervising *against* students the atmosphere was considerably more serious in tone, more formal and methodical; the supervisors confronted the students, thus dissolving the learning alliance (which, however, could soon be re-constituted to form a new learning alliance).

When supervising *with* students, the shared explorative thinking is observed to be creative, unpredictable and somewhat 'chaotic' in nature, having no fixed endpoint and often becoming sidetracked into unplanned topics. It can even lead supervisors and students down blind alleys, where they have to backtrack to return to the original topic of discussion. When supervising *against* students the discussion becomes more scripted and linear, often following the notes and feedback prepared by the supervisor, which are dealt with serially. This is observed to give structure and direction to the meetings, which often seemed to be lacking or perhaps unwanted when supervising *with* students. When supervising *with* students the language use itself was observed several times to acquire a more experimental nature, playing with new possible ways of conceptualizing or describing what appeared in the data material. This experimental language from both supervisors and students sometimes caused laughter and giddiness in the dialogues. When supervising *against* students the language of both supervisors and students was more controlled, more reflective and restrained; the form of delivery becomes a graver matter, and more precautions are taken in order to balance the critical comments delivered either way.

	Supervising "with" students (process)	Supervising "against" students (product)
Purpose	Explorative, collaborative	Evaluative, text feedback
Roles (relations)	Symmetrical, dialogue	Asymmetrical, monologue
Atmosphere	Humorous, playful	Serious, methodical
Style of thinking	Unpredictable, chaotic	Scripted, linear
Language	Experimental, giddy	Controlled, restrained

Figure 1

To transfer these findings into the role vocabulary offered in the literature, as described earlier in this book, process supervision or supervising *with* students, overlaps with the supervisor roles of the colleague, coach and friend. Similarly, product supervision, supervising *against* students, overlaps with the supervisor roles of the teacher, master and mentor. However, it is an important point that the schema above is not about particular roles, but the underlying core pedagogy from which such roles develop. This shows that the supervisor and student roles presented from the earliest days of research into doctoral supervision represent different ways that supervisors tackle and respond to the two core theatrical aspects of doctoral supervision: supervising *with* and *against* students. Each specific role, for example the role of the supervisor as a mentor, is a pedagogical 'knot' that unites ideas about how to think, act, feel, and respond to the particular doctoral student. If you assume the role of the mentor you find a certain balance in the with/against ambivalence that constitutes a central part of the particular doctoral supervisor's pedagogical approach. The supervisor and student roles can in this light be viewed as 'pedagogical monads', supervisory microcosms, through which people relate, teach and learn – but these may switch many times during one meeting, so they are not static, as shown by Gatfield (2005), and they build upon very different pedagogical ideals and preconceptions, as shown by Lee (2008; 2012). The reason for this rather abstract concept of role-theatrics is to lay bare not merely the more or less generic system of roles and related pedagogical strategies – this has been done before – but to show that roles and relations are not a point of departure, but the point where supervisors arrive as a personal and professional response to the fundamental challenge of the with/against ambivalence of doctoral pedagogy.

4.0.3 Role-theatrics and ambivalence

Ambivalence in doctoral supervision and pedagogy is not a problem to be solved, but a condition for role making that should be accepted and respected. With the findings of my own study reflected against the findings in the research literature more broadly, I conclude that ambivalence is at the heart of doctoral pedagogy. The roles in doctoral supervision become manifest in supervision practice, and thus visible to researchers, because the relation between supervisors and students is a *pedagogical* relation. The doctoral students want, and need, to learn how to prepare, design, conduct and analyze research projects on their own, but the supervisor is also present, not to solve the challenging issues for the student, but to assist him and to guide him when needed. What form this guidance takes depends on each new instance of individual supervision processes. Doctoral pedagogy consists of this ambivalence between the supervisor learning *with* the student, and evaluating the student's work *against* the student's own will and opinion. I do not apply the term 'ambivalence' to describe a problem with, a flaw in or a dysfunctional element of doctoral pedagogy; I aim at the meaning of doubleness, and maybe even contradiction, which is inherent in doctoral pedagogy and one of the main drivers in the supervisor and student relationship. Ambivalence is necessary for supervisors and students to be able to reflect on their own roles, and thus also their own teaching and learning approaches, as well as their own understanding of quality in doctoral work. Supervisors should embrace this ambivalence and see the many different roles as possible ways of managing and dealing with it in a pedagogically sound way. However, it also means that there are new possibilities for roles we have not yet heard of, which must be sought and explored in order for doctoral pedagogy to enhance the quality of PhD research.

This said, ambivalence must be acknowledged as the ground for several generic challenges in the doctoral supervision process. For example, sometimes the supervisor and student roles do not match, and the student applies a learning strategy as a 'colleague' only for the supervisor to respond in the role of the 'teacher'. Or it can happen the other way around – the supervisor expects the student to assume the role of the 'colleague' but the student clings to the role of the 'student'. Problems can also be caused when the roles are not played out but abandoned halfway through, casting their unresolved shadows into the new roles assumed and the new relationship taken up. As Green (2005) has noted this may create "unfinished business" when ideals and expectations for the supervision process are thought to have been changed or renegotiated, but still haunt the supervisory relationship because of hurt feelings or unfulfilled expectations. When the ambivalence of doctoral supervision is not balanced out with the appropriate role-work and a role-making process, the supervisory relationship may be caught up in what Cherry calls the "paradox and fog of supervision" (2012).

Thus, this study probes the foundation for Gatfield's (2005) dynamic role model and Lee's (2008; 2012) role framework. I argue that it is because of an underlying ambivalence in doctoral pedagogy that roles can change over time, allowing for new learning and teaching approaches. Because of the ambivalent nature of doctoral supervision supervisors and students have the opportunity to revisit, reconsider and alter their roles and the supervisory relationship, which has many advantages despite the sometimes demanding pedagogical work that awaits the supervisor when roles change drastically during the PhD (Grant 1999; 2003; 2005). When a new role is assumed by the supervisor or student, their relationship may change, meaning the pedagogy changes accordingly because of the new conditions for role-work and the inherent learning and teaching strategies in this role-work. The deep link between relational and intellectual dimensions thus becomes visible once more: The way the supervisor and student understand the nature of the research in question is inextricably linked to the way they understand their roles as doctoral supervisors and students, as well as the form of supervisory relationship they perform through the research process – or the way the research is conducted against the backdrop of the role-work happening between them. The good supervisor should be mindful of the dynamic character of the roles and relations in the supervisory dyad or team, and of how the nature of the research, and the epistemological ideals inherent in it, are influenced, and influence, the roles and the relationship during the supervision process. Because of the ambivalence inherent in doctoral pedagogy, supervision constitutes the link between relational and intellectual levels, which lie at the core of doctoral pedagogy.

4.1 SUBTLE PEDAGOGY

Building on the findings presented in chapters two and three, I formulate 'subtlety' as the second defining element of doctoral supervision as an advanced pedagogy. In contrast to all other forms of supervision at the university, doctoral supervision meetings do not only focus on the assignment or thesis, but are constantly being 'interrupted' by discussion of institutional matters, conference participation, choices between PhD courses and generally how to maintain overview and balance in the long and demanding process of the PhD. Therefore, supervisors cannot be said to apply just one form of doctoral pedagogy – they continuously switch between many different pedagogies depending on the specific theme emerging from within the meeting as a whole. Doctoral pedagogy can thus be characterized as a subtle pedagogy.

4.1.1 Multiple levels, multiple pedagogies

Doctoral pedagogy and supervision today are being researched and described as a multilayered phenomenon, in which one of the most important tasks for supervisors is to support and guide students navigating the often complex organizational structures consisting of multiple interwoven "nested contexts" (McAlpine & Norton 2006). Many different requirements are made of doctoral students during their PhD; they are expected not only to conduct original and valid scientific work, but also to complete a range of often demanding PhD courses, to take on teaching and supervision tasks, to learn how to navigate the review system when publishing papers for the first time, to be part of a larger academic team with senior researchers, to establish international networks and to be stationed abroad on the sometimes obligatory research stay.

Borrowing three metaphors from Catherine Manathung'as study on interdisciplinary research (Manathunga 2009), and applying them to doctoral education, this organizational hybridity can be disclosed further. Being part of this organizational hybrid-space demands students to develop "[i]ntercultural attributes, such as tolerance of ambiguity, flexibility and trust" in order to "deal with epistemological, theoretical, linguistic and methodological diversity" (Manathunga 2009: 136). The first metaphor Manathunga offers is that of the "butterfly"; doctoral students, when navigating the complex organizational set-up, "are always in-between, flitting here and there, never settling for too long, but the productive aspect of this liminality lies in its potential for creating new identities and knowledge" (Manathunga 2009: 138). To use Manathunga's second metaphor, this organizational complexity may result in the individual doctoral student's PhD turning into a "mongrel scholarship", forcing the student to assume "a destabilized identity but one that pulls together different perspectives and is, therefore, open to change and growth" (Manathunga 2009: 140); this also demands a particularly sensitive and dynamic form of doctoral pedagogy on the supervisor's part. In the terms of Manathunga's third metaphor, the doctoral student may sometimes have to assume the features of a "chameleon" as the multilayered educational challenges mean they must "select several hues of their new disciplinary [and organizational] environment to blend in with the new ways of thinking and being" (Manathunga 2009: 142). The supervisor is similarly presented with the pedagogical task of adopting a variety of approaches in order to create the necessary variety in the supervisory dialogue.

Similar points are made by the authors of the comprehensive book on socialization in doctoral education edited by Gardner and Mendoza (2010). In this book Golde (2010) describes how doctoral students are "entering different worlds" (Golde 2010: 79) depending on the disciplinary communities they may come to belong to. McDaniels (2010) describes the range of skills needed by the doctoral student who also becomes a teacher for the first time: conceptual understanding, knowledge skills, interpersonal skills and the ability to work with his own attitudes and habits when engaging with students in a complex setting that has many different stakeholders such as the doctoral student himself, the faculty members, the department, the university and potentially also external agencies involved in the course programme. And these are just the skills the student needs to acquire for teaching. When it comes to conducting the actual research, Weidman (2010) states that the individual doctoral student is confronted with yet more challenges. He needs to the develop research skills outlined by the doctoral programme he belongs to; he must participate as a 'trainee' in the research projects managed by the senior researchers in the department; he must consider the financial support for his research; and he must balance faculty and peer interaction in his research project together with the feedback, and criticism, given by groups of mentors and advisers. Doctoral students must "learn to negotiate the demands placed upon them in order to fulfill expectations, primarily by faculty, for building a portfolio of research accomplishments necessary for the type of careers graduates are seeking" (Weidman 2010: 52).

As argued by Danby and Lee (2012), traditional understandings of the relational aspects of doctoral supervision that include only the supervisor–student relationship "must be modified if it is to account for the complex relations at the heart of doctoral learning. In particular, the learner, the teacher and their co-produced knowledge are not the only 'agencies' that contribute to pedagogy; they also interact with the academic discipline" (Danby & Lee 2012: 4-5). The discipline is always an "invisible presence" (Danby & Lee 2012: 5) in supervision settings, and "doctoral pedagogy is best understood 'eco-socially' in terms of a total environment in which knowledge and identities are co-produced" (ibid.). Danby and Lee outline a 'doctoral ecology' (my term) that reveals that a holistic view of doctoral pedagogy, in which all of the different organizational layers are aligned in one comprehensive system, may not be possible. In line with Gatfield's (2005) point that the supervisor and student roles and relations change over time, the larger organizational layers of doctoral pedagogy can be said to contain a similar dynamism:

> As an antidote to the individualising of the experience of the doctoral student dominant in much of the literature, the concept of design draws attention to regularities, patterns, freedoms and constraints that are so-

cially produced, and produced as the accomplishment of ongoing actions, rather than as a predetermined and fixed design. What this means is that attention is given to the ordinary work practices or 'doings' of doctoral work, as accomplished within social domains. (Danby & Lee 2012: 6)

The above must be seen in combination with all the 'non-formal' (see chapter two, section 2.2) parameters of everyday doctoral education, as powerfully invoked in the study by Jazvac-Martez, Chen & McAlpine (2011), where it is found that "[d]epartments and academics generally were seen to be lacking in awareness of the complexity of students' past and present lives beyond the academy. To the students, there appeared to be no institutional oversight of practices and structures to support them, leaving them feeling relatively without power in the department" (Jazvac-Martez, Chen & McAlpine 2011: 31). This demands sensitivity to issues of personal, even private, character that supervisors must in some way bring up during the supervision meetings if they are felt to influence that students' progression in a negative way. The authors argue that the relational aspect of doctoral supervision should not only refer to the interpersonal supervisor–student relationship, but to include the individual student's relations to the many different layers of the organizational set up, and even the relations between the different organizational layers that are not directly linked to the student's project, but nevertheless often implicitly influence the student's work on a daily basis. This suggests that student agency should be accorded a broader meaning when discussing doctoral pedagogy. In this light doctoral students are perceived as "active agents [that] contribute and respond to the dynamics of social life" (Jazvac-Martez, Chen & McAlpine 2011: 22). This calls for a doctoral pedagogy, or a variety of possible doctoral pedagogies, that can help the student mediate and navigate the highly complex organizational environment of the PhD.

4.1.2. Wielding multiplicities

My Observations of doctoral supervision meetings showed that it does not make much sense to say that *one* individual supervision meeting was taking place, but more that the one individual meeting was actually a cluster of meetings within meetings within meetings. As argued in chapter three, section 3.0.2, not one, but multiple, dialogues were taking place simultaneously during a single meeting. This highlights the character of doctoral supervision meetings as a multilayered pedagogical event with several agendas, and several purposes and possible learning outcomes. During the observed meetings many aspects of the doctoral educational context were addressed serially or in parallel, and I have categorized the different topics and sub-topics in four main categories, which apply to all the meetings observed (see also Figure 2 below):

- *Institution* Courses, conferences, evaluation logs, teaching, stay abroad
- *Discipline* Concepts, research literature, theory, methodology
- *Design* Research process, data collection, data processing, analysis
- *Process* Organizing work, coping, peer networks, private sphere

All of these topics were in play during the observed meetings. Some played a larger part in some meetings than others, but they all figured in the content of the meetings, if only momentarily. What was interesting was that the topics mentioned were not dealt with in a structured way, and some were never part of the original agenda presented at the beginning of the meeting, which was mostly set by the supervisor, but in some cases also by the student. As described in chapter three, section 3.0.2, the topics discussed were sometimes brought into the dialogue spontaneously by way of association – as when, for example, a discussion about finishing up a certain chapter in the thesis containing a particular concluding point led the student to ask if he could take this point up in a conference that he and the supervisor would attend together. This furthermore led the supervisor to ask if the paper the student was writing for that conference could be published as part of the thesis. Finishing up the discussion about aligning the conference presentation and the possible journal article, the dialogue might return to the initial topic about the supervisor giving feedback on the student's draft version of a chapter for his thesis. Such skipping between topics was observed in all the meetings. The rhythm and pace could be different, and the meetings could be more or less structured or chaotic, but they all contained these spontaneous changes of direction. Sub-topics suddenly presented themselves from mental, or discursive, places that were invisible to the participants initially, and like 'wormholes' or gateways between horizons they allowed the supervisor and student to plunge into different dialogical spaces and back out again, or continue on into new spaces.

	Institution	Discipline	Design	Process
Within the same meeting	Courses, conferences, teaching, etc.	Concepts, literature, theory, etc.	Research process, data collection	Organizing work, coping, peer networks, etc.

Figure 2

It was also interesting to observe the way the supervisor and student roles, and the implicit pedagogy in this relation, changed when the topic changed. When the dialogue centered around 'institutional' matters, as for example course or conference participation, or planning teaching (see Figure 2), the supervisor would assume the role of the teacher – directing the student toward what the supervisor thought was the most fruitful way to approach matters based on her extensive experience and knowledge about the institutional matters discussed. When the dialogue focused on disciplinary matters, the supervisor and student would typically become mutually engaged; the role of the supervisor would change from that of the teacher to the colleague, or mentor, taking a visibly less directional and more symmetrical and collaborative approach to the matters addressed. When the dialogue addressed 'design' aspects, the supervisor role would change to that of the mentor, withdrawing from the role of the colleague, but not returning to that of the teacher. When discussing 'design' aspects the student would often consult with the supervisor, asking for her advice. When the dialogue turned to process-related issues the supervisor would typically take on the role of the coach, and in a few cases the role of the friend; the student played the starring role, and the supervisors were very cautious not to be directive but to be as supportive they could in the more withdrawn position of the coach.

These observations showed that the topics addressed, the roles assumed and the pedagogies applied were all deeply interlinked, and that when one of these elements changed in the dialogues, the others changed as well. This meant that the doctoral students and supervisors sometimes assumed several roles during a single meeting, which made visible not only the dialogical complexity of the meetings, as described in chapter three, but also a pedagogical complexity with implications for the students' learning outcomes. The supervisors were observed to have all of these topics and sub-topics, and even their interrelatedness, active on standby, ready to engage in, and often to initiate, a sub-topic related to the main topic addressed. The supervisors could intuitively grasp the interrelated character of the four topic categories shown in Figure 2 above, and had no apparent difficulty in changing spontaneously from discussing the individual doctoral student's conference paper one moment to suddenly bridging this thread to a weak link in the student's research process discussed maybe a month before. For the supervisors this complexity was intuitively managed and wielded, and the changes in pace and topic seemed to come naturally to them. In this way the doctoral supervisors could be said to have a 'multi-perspective' on the dialogue, seeing into different topics and worlds simultaneously. The students, on the other hand, were observed to think from within one topic at a time, from a 'mono-perspective', and typically they would not make as many spontaneous leaps into new topics as the supervisors. The students often struggled – constructively – to gain a sometimes slippery footing on one platform in the dialogue at a time. The more experienced students were not as easily put out or confused by the supervisors' sudden change of direction in the dialogue as the newer ones were. However, these newer students were clearly not as used to, and probably not as interested in, the sudden changes in dialogue, direction and topic.

This finding shows that doctoral supervisors have a tacit and intuitive grasp of the underlying structure, patterns and fabric of the supervisory dialogue and how the topics interrelate. This lays bare what Hockey almost twenty years ago called the supervisor's "craft" (Hockey 1997). Two of Hockey's characteristics of the supervisor craft are what he calls "foreseeing" and "timing" (ibid.). This corresponds well to the findings of my observations, in the sense that the doctoral supervisors always seemed to be one step ahead of the doctoral students in the dialogue. They often intuitively grasped the link to topics that naturally seemed to succeed whatever they were discussing at the moment, and they timed the change of topic with a high degree of precision and relevance, when they felt it was ripe for change, expansion or development. This form of wielding, maybe even juggling, the complexity of the links between topics showed significant dialogical know-how on the supervisors' part; it reminds one of supervisory acrobatics or artistry – in the sense that it might seem highly difficult from the outside, but for the supervisors it seemed to be the most natural thing in the world. However, the students, all except some of the most advanced and experienced ones, did not master the supervision craft, and they seemed more taken aback, and sometimes confused, when the supervisors performed one of these 'stunts' of, for example, making a topic about the challenge of organizing the data collection into an opportunity to stay at an internationally esteemed university for a longer period of the PhD. It raises the question of whether or not doctoral supervisors *should* make a connection between topics, just because they *could* perform that link, or whether they should shield their students from some of complexity and its immanent pedagogical imperatives.

4.1.3 Subtlety as organizational and pedagogical glue

On the background of my study, what can be said to be missing in John Hockey's framework of the supervisor's craft, for example, is the 'pedagogical subtlety' in doctoral supervision. I argue that subtlety is one of the five essential aspects of the advanced pedagogy that defines doctoral supervision. Pedagogical subtlety is what glues together the organizational complexity explored in chapter two and the dialogical 'multi-intentionality' explored in chapter three. It links organizational and dialogical planes together in a unified and robust doctoral pedagogy. The pedagogical characteristic of subtlety means that the supervisors weave institutional (organizational), disciplinary (epistemological) and personal (existential) dimensions of the students' learning processes together, making doctoral education habitable as a world with several sub-worlds, or dimensions, that need to be correlated and aligned for the students during the PhD. This does not mean that the supervisors assume a 'godlike' view during supervision meetings, but that they have the skill to enter, leave, re-enter and generally move between different organizational and dialogical perspectives and mindsets relevant to the different kinds of equally important, but not always aligned, dimensions of doctoral education.

Pedagogical subtlety in doctoral supervision is the ability to see corridors between the institutional, disciplinary and personal dimensions of the educational process, which may dim, hidden or caught in a blind angle for the doctoral student. Subtlety is a powerful pedagogical feature as, when successfully performed with sensitivity, skill and care, it balances many different educational levels of the PhD, and supports the student through many different potential challenges in the learning process. Pedagogical subtlety is the ability to travel inside distinct educational perspectives and see the world from within that singular perspective, then leave it and sink into another. If this is not done skillfully the doctoral supervisor risks tossing the student around the ring, taking up too much space and possibly pushing the student outside the dialogue. As observed during supervision meetings, the student might respond to an exaggerated organizational complexity with confusion, insecurity and even anger because of the feeling of losing control both in the conversation and in the overall project. Subtle pedagogy is therefore necessary, using the student's perspective as the default for the supervisory dialogue – the base from which other perspectives may be sought. Subtlety in doctoral supervision is about letting the supervisor perspective be submerged within the student perspective, which in many ways draws this form of pedagogy close to the process of active listening, described in chapter three, section 3.2.1. Subtlety in doctoral supervision relies on a particular form of distance from the student's project. The supervisor has the luxury of becoming submerged within the individual educational aspect of the student's many-sided learning process, but without the same form of obligation as the student himself. They thus have the opportunity to play with these different organizational dimensions, since they can more easily detach and disconnect themselves and resurface from time to time to gain an overall view of their interrelatedness. This does not mean that the supervisor should take less responsibility and care than the student does. It means a different challenge is presented to the supervisor when engaging in the complexity of balancing and navigating the different educational planes of the PhD in supervision settings. It demands strong relational skills as the supervisor, as shown above, should always be mindful of how the roles and relations shift when turning to different organizational dimensions of the PhD. It also requires advanced communication skills as the supervisor must select what to say and what not to say, as well as knowing how to linguistically mark out when and why the shifts are happening. Pedagogical subtlety can sometimes look deceptively easy from the outside, but it is a highly demanding and challenging feature to wield in practice.

4.2 STRANGE PEDAGOGY

Building on the findings of chapters two and three, 'strangeness' may be formulated as the third defining element of doctoral supervision as an advanced pedagogy. 'Strangeness' is at the heart of the pedagogical aspect of doctoral supervision. It is present in the interwoven pedagogical fabric of structure and direction on the one side and labyrinthine and chaotic intuition and idiosyncrasy on the other. Doctoral supervision is a strange pedagogy as both the generic and idiosyncratic dimensions were observed to be of key importance to doctoral supervisors and students' intentions and ambitions for creating a fruitful shared thought space.

4.2.1 The alien force within doctoral supervision

The differences in doctoral supervisors' and students' understandings of the research endeavor undertaken in the PhD are often "tied to disciplinary differences" (Pearson & Brew 2002: 145). However, one of the most interesting findings in Pearson and Brew's (2002) empirical study on the conception of scholarship in doctoral supervision is that despite all the generic- and disciplinary-dependent conditions for good communication during supervision meetings, it is still not possible to ensure alignment and mutual understanding in supervisory dialogues. They state that:

> Individuals' conceptions of research are a function of a complex set of factors, of which disciplinary allegiance is only one. (...) researchers carrying out similar kinds of research – for example, laboratory-based research, collaborative team-based research, individualized investigations – did not necessarily share the same conceptions. (...) It means that the supervisor cannot assume that the student has the same idea as himself or herself about what they are doing when they are carrying out research. (Pearson & Brew 2002: 145)

Despite working together closely during doctoral supervision processes, it may difficult for supervisors to really know and understand their students' "raw dream of what higher education might mean for them as individuals" (Batchelor 2008: 52). As Halse points out, as in any other form of practice-based work "the nitty-gritty of learning to 'do' doctoral supervision [happens] through negotiated practice 'on the job'" (Halse 2011: 568). Seen in this light doctoral supervision is relatively unknowable and what it means to be a doctoral supervisor is for the individual supervisor herself to discover along the way. Halse sheds light on an often overlooked aspect of doctoral supervision – the supervisor's learning journey. While doctoral supervision might feel like a slippery or hazy process at times for students, it is also a learning process for supervisors. What it means to be a doctoral supervisor, and what form(s) of pedagogy the individual supervisor applies in different stages of that learning process, changes as the supervisor's self-image changes. Halse suggests, along with Barnett (2007), Barnett and Coate (2006) and Batchelor (2006; 2008), that the focus on "becoming" must be foregrounded, and that "supervisors' learning experiences shape their subjectivities and identities, and that supervision is an ongoing ontological process of 'becoming a supervisor'" (Halse 2011: 557).

In supervision settings, doctoral supervisors find it difficult – although perhaps not in the same ways as their students – "to translate their intuitive knowledge into concrete form, and to communicate this new knowledge in ways that [are] comprehensible and productive for students" (Halse 2011: 567). It can be an entirely different challenge to convey knowledge to students in supervision settings, as opposed to conveying the same knowledge to other researchers at conferences, or to colleagues in the coffee room, and to submit it to scientific journals. As Halse has shown in her empirical study, the knowledge articulated, formed and shaped in supervisory dialogues might be entirely different from the forms of knowledge generated in other spheres of everyday academic work. She suggests that we "recognize that valuable and meaningful knowledge is generated through the practice of doctoral supervision, and that this has a significant impact on 'becoming a supervisor' and on 'supervision as becoming'" (Halse 2011: 569). This posits a link between the shaping of knowledge and the shaping of the supervisor identity: Knowledge work in doctoral supervision is also identity work. As Cherry describes, in doctoral supervision,we "meet *ourselves*, not only the world we think we are exploring. Our own personas, our personal histories, our values and motives are inevitably and actively engaged – some would say embedded – in the essence of research [supervision]" (Cherry 2012: 9, my italics). Supervision takes place "in the complex, always unique 'between' space [which can be called] the zone of transformation" (Cherry 2012: 12). My point is to stress that deep within the formal institutionalized framework for doctoral education, and on the underside of strong disciplinary norms and habits for doctoral supervision that exist within particular departments or fields of research, there exists an *alien space*, or an alien force, that constantly threatens and destabilizes the premises for supervision.

Grant (2010) makes a similar point in that supervision meetings consist of improvised dialogues that are fragile because they "occur on the edge of chaos and incoherence" (Grant 2010: 281). No matter how well planned and structured supervision meetings are, and no matter how skilled and experienced the supervisor is, the dialogue is always to some extent 'flawed' by misunderstandings, things unheard or wrongly understood, trivial interruptions by phones or colleagues and improvised trains of thought that may be hard both to articulate and to follow. Grant writes that improvised dialogues in research supervision are made up of:

> trial and error, of unpredictable remembering and forgetting, of unreasonable inspiration and aridity, of clarity and confusion, of articulateness and fumbling speech, of arguments that come to fruition and those that do not, and of testing one's ideas out with others and thus facing the danger of showing oneself to be a dull or flaky thinker. (Grant 2010: 283)

This points to the strange but also "vibrant moment in supervision" (Grant 2010: 284), which discloses doctoral supervision as a "disciplined yet playful sociality of thinking together, exploring ideas, bouncing them off others, following a train of thought, being infected by another's enthusiasm, taking challenges and rising to meet them, coming to ideas you might never have come to alone" (ibid.). On the same lines as Grant, Bengtsen (2012) argues that this 'alien force' of doctoral supervision, though dependent on the personal perspectives of supervisors and students, exists pedagogically as a *relational* and not a subject-specific phenomenon. It is because of the supervision *meeting* between supervisor and student that the potential for new and unforeseen knowledge work arises. In addition, as argued by Bengtsen in the following quotation, this alien force, or 'pedagogical idiosyncrasy' as I call it in my doctoral thesis, is not an element of chaos to be feared or shunned, but a necessary element for creativity and originality, which helps propel the pedagogical event towards closure:

> Every single supervisory dialogue has its own pedagogical idiosyncrasy; its own pedagogical causality and its own particular mixture of personality and professionalism. This form of pedagogical logic, or imperative, is particularly interesting as it cannot be made universal or general (...). In spite of the general pedagogical elements that can be seen to be present across supervision meetings, this study shows that supervisory dialogues also close up and disappear into their own pedagogical worlds. This is not to say that every supervision meeting is a form of pedagogical solipsism, in which only the supervisor and student know what is going on. Instead, the individual supervisory dialogue takes place *because of* this closing-up-around-itself. (Bengtsen 2012: 177, my translation)

The doctoral supervision meeting can thus be said to be a learning event for supervisors and students alike. One of the main challenges of doctoral supervision is to understand the deep link between how a person changes during the demanding tasks of the PhD and how *thoughts change*. Thought is more than an intellectual-epistemological phenomenon in doctoral supervision; it must be understood ontologically, not only as something that persons have, but also as an element in its own right.

4.2.2 The strange duality between structure and chaos

Each supervision meeting progressed on two main planes – a generic plane and an idiosyncratic plane. Both planes seem equally important to the doctoral supervisors and students, but they are nevertheless categorically different dimensions of the supervision meeting. This duality between ordering, structuring, jointly aligning and balancing the dialogue between supervisor and student on the one side, and the cut up, erratic, individual and sometimes even egoistic relational epistemology and pedagogy on the other side, belongs at the core of doctoral pedagogy. Both pedagogical dimensions were observed across all the studied supervision meetings, like an intentionally schizophrenic play of thoughts. This pedagogical duality was observed to play out most strongly in relation to the following four forms of supervision practice:

- *Meeting structure*   How meetings progressed by moving towards closure
- *Topics*   How topics were presented and became part of meetings
- *Thinking space*   How different ideas/arguments functioned in meetings
- *Form of dialogue*   The degree of contact present in the communication

In the generic dimension of supervision practice the meetings observed progressed from a point of departure marked by an introduction or presentation of the agenda for the meeting, from either the supervisor or the student. As described in the section above, meetings could contain all sorts of interwoven themes and sub-agendas, but nevertheless they were kept moving when the supervisor, or in some cases the student, signaled that a specific topic had been dealt with sufficiently. This direction in the dialogue moved inevitably towards some form of closure in the end. The supervisors and students were both constantly aware of the underlying agenda, and the fact that there were central issues that needed to be managed and discussed before the end of the meeting. This gave meetings a linear framing and direction. At the same time, the meeting structure was constantly being disturbed and broken by ideas, comments, rememberings and associations that sidetracked the discussion and fragmented the dialogue, as also pointed out in chapter three, section 3.0.2. This labyrinthine character of the meeting structure seemed to dissolve the sense of progression, and left a more chaotic mark on the dialogue that was oftentimes tackled with sub-themes and incomplete dialogical patterns. In this way every supervision meeting also had a 'non-structure', or a non-structural element, which seemed to work within the overall framing structure. This was mirrored in the form of dialogue, which on the generic level followed a conversational rhythm of turn-taking and mutual recognition. On the idiosyncratic level, however, the dialogue could be said to be dislocated, fragmented and 'discordant' in the sense that supervisors and students did not always know how to connect with the other person's change of rhythm and pattern when the labyrinthine structure 'flooded' the linear meeting structure.

A similar tendency was observed regarding the topics presented and discussed during the meetings. The planned meeting structure naturally contained topics to be addressed at different stages, so the planned topics were introduced during the parts of the meeting that followed the agenda. During the non-structured parts of the meeting, new topics were brought in that emerged by way of association and inspiration. These improvised topics were spontaneously generated and could take up a greater or smaller part of the overall meeting depending on how much potential they were judged to have by the supervisor and student together. This disclosed two forms of thinking spaces during the meetings. On the one hand a shared, collaborative thinking space was created whenever the planned topics were addressed, because these seemed to refer to an educational, and academic, contract, or codex – meaning that supervisors and students were obliged to address planned and agreed upon topics. However, whenever the improvised topics were introduced into the meeting either by the supervisor or the student, these seemed to emerge from intuitive and personal thinking spaces. These thinking spaces could be said to be partly hidden as the point of origin was often blurred, and not before they were introduced into the shared thinking space of the jointly agreed upon topical part of the dialogue did these more personal thinking spaces become visible. These observations are organized into a schematic overview in Figure 3:

	Meeting structure	Topics	Thinking space	Form of dialogue
Generic	Progression, linear, direction	Planned, prepared,	Shared, collaborative	Aligned, rhythm, turn-taking, stable
Idiosyncratic	Labyrinthine, non-linear, chaotic	Improvised, spontaneous, emerging	Personal, intuitive, hidden	Dislocated, fragmented, discordant

Figure 3

The pedagogical implications, or teaching and learning strategies, that emerge from this so-called duality between structure and chaos in supervision meetings are manifold. First, supervisors and students at times disappeared into their own personal and idiosyncratic thinking and learning spaces and became obscure to each other. When occupying such deeply personalized thinking spaces, which could last from seconds to minutes, supervisors and students were observed to be searching for each other in thought, action and speech. This was witnessed in the dialogue, which suddenly changed from progression and a lucent flow into a blindfolded conversation, where it was difficult to see the next step, and supervisors and students momentarily lost control over the dialogue and the shared thought space. However, this forcing of the structure to breaking point seemed to be a key component of the good supervisory dialogue, and the power and ability to let ideas and topics emerge spontaneously, and by way of association and 'thought-links', proved to be the sign of a tacit and mutually sought after learning experience within the meeting.

4.2.3 Strangeness makes possible creativity in thought

The conversational patterns of doctoral supervision meetings are at times chaotic and arabesque. When supervisors and students retreat into their own inner thought spaces and hidden epistemological reservoirs they sometimes never find each other again on the particular line of thought they set out on, but need to build up momentum in the dialogue once more. At other times they connected in impressively advanced and sophisticated ways by modulating their own idiosyncratic lines of thought to the shared thinking space and joint dialogue. I argue that this dialogical and pedagogical dissonance is not a flaw in supervision pedagogy on either the supervisors' or the students' side, but a willed and intentional pressure put on the dialogue itself in order to test it, to harness its power and to make it break only to come back to life with even more rigour and force than before. A core feature of doctoral pedagogy is the shared ability and ambition between supervisors and students to willingly make the dialogue between them frail and insecure.

This feature is sometimes mistaken for a form of 'criticality' in doctoral pedagogy, but I do not see it this way. What is at stake here is a core feature of doctoral pedagogy to do with a willed lack of control and intentional 'thought crash'. The dialogue only breaks when the shared thought crashes. This 'strange' feature of doctoral pedagogy makes us realize that supervision is not only about criticality and harnessing the arguments and research designs of doctoral work, but also and simultaneously showing the vulnerability of one's own thought and exposing the weakest parts of the thesis, in an almost ruthless manner. Using Grant's (2010) trope of the eggshell to reflect the findings of my own study, a new dimension of doctoral pedagogy emerges. It shows supervision as something tangible, almost corporeal, something to be used and used up (Lingis 1998). To be in doctoral supervision – to bring oneself into this pedagogical space – is to risk one's own ideas and work. It is to wear one's best work down, to make use of it even though it may be broken and damaged in the process, so that one must throw it away afterwards.

Another way to capture this 'strange' dimension of doctoral pedagogy is to compare it with the imagery of pot-holing found in Barnett (2015b) and Bengtsen and Barnett (2015). It is like travelling through a dark cave system and suddenly arriving in a cavern where light streams in from cracks in the walls. This image illustrates how the supervisors and students worked within their own systems of thought, trying to move towards each other even though they did not know the way, but "always hopeful that it [was] worth pressing on, even in the darkness" (Barnett 2015b: 9). Biesta's point (Biesta 2006) about "natality" as a core feature of pedagogical work, drawn from Hannah Arendt, is also relevant here. The condition of natality refers to "[a]ction as beginning, (...) the fact of birth, because with each birth something 'uniquely new' comes into the world" (Biesta 2006: 81). Strangeness in doctoral supervision does not correlate only with the idiosyncratic aspects of supervision that constitute misunderstandings. The point is that strangeness makes generic *and* idiosyncratic dimensions visible and available for reflection because strangeness is the very outcome of this paradox inscribed on the inside of doctoral supervision practice.

The pedagogy of strangeness in doctoral supervision reveals two central issues. First, secrecy and idiosyncrasy play a greater role in the performance of doctoral supervision than is often acknowledged in discourses about quality assurance and professionalization of doctoral education. This is not a romantic or nostalgic point about safeguarding every supervisor's or student's own inner being and protecting it from further inquiry. Actually the opposite is the case here. I argue that we need to understand better the workings of these idiosyncratic aspects that seem so essentially linked to the creative and explorative nature of doctoral supervision and research supervision more generally. Second, a peculiar notion of *trust* is emerging. This is not the traditional trust between supervisor and student as persons relating to each other in a professional setting. It is a trust between supervisors and students and *thought itself*. Supervisors and students can only be so daring in their exploration of the range and scope of their research because they trust that their knowledge-work will not be lost or emptied out. Doctoral supervisors and students use up every means of thought available to them when engaging in supervision; they combust thoughts and at the same time trust in the abundance of thought available to them. The constant pressure supervisors and students put on the potential of thought discloses an often overlooked feature of doctoral supervision: that the assumption that thought and thought-work is unlimited in scope is a necessary premise for creativity of thought, argument and research design.

4.3 EMBEDDED PEDAGOGY

Building on the findings of chapter two, section 2.3, where it is shown that core disciplinary threshold concepts influence supervision pedagogy, and chapter three, sections 3.2.1 and 3.2.2, which deal with the merging of pedagogy, epistemology, voice and thought, I formulate 'embeddedness' as the fourth defining element of doctoral supervision as an advanced pedagogy. I argue that doctoral pedagogy is embedded deeply within disciplinary concerns and doctoral research processes. This embeddedness seems to be both a great strength of the pedagogy encompassing doctoral supervision *and* one of the least accessible forms of pedagogy for an outsider researcher or educational developer.

4.3.1 The link between subject matter and pedagogy

During the PhD students encounter many thresholds to be crossed. Forming an identity as an independent researcher is a demanding and complex process, and as shown in chapter two this is only one of many parallel challenges that await the doctoral student. Although much focus today within doctoral education research and development is being directed towards areas outside the core disciplinary aspects of doctoral supervision (see e.g. chapter 2, section 2.1 and 2.2), Kiley (2009), Kiley and Wisker (2009) and Wisker and Robinson (2009) remind us of the fact that doctoral students, and their supervisors, to a very large extent see doctoral supervision as a disciplinary undertaking that has the primary goal of contributing new and powerful knowledge to a given field of research. When doctoral students experience difficulties in their research process and are "stuck, that is, unable to progress and yet realizing there is 'something' that they need to understand but cannot quite grasp" (Kiley 2009: 296), they interpret this as a disciplinary problem – to do with theoretical knowledge that might be incomplete, or a flaw in the research design or methodological set-up of their study. In this way, doctoral students address and approach lack of progress in their research as a lack of knowledge, skills or competences. This is highlighted in Kiley's empirical study:

> It is not uncommon for learners, prior to full understanding, to mimic the language and behaviours they consider appropriate for the understanding with which they are struggling. It is even possible for some undergraduate students to graduate still not really understanding some of the major concepts underpinning that discipline. At the research education level mimicry is often adapted explicitly as a way of inducting learners into their new environment, for example, through engagement in seminars where they can learn how to ask questions and pose issues in ways which are appropriate to the level and discipline. (Kiley 2009: 296)

We need to understand more fully the deep link between progression in the PhD on disciplinary *and* personal levels, and we need to be more precise in our descriptions of supervision as a relational pedagogy, since empirical studies show that relational teaching and supervision relies heavily on working with core concepts and deep epistemological structures and levels inherent in the specific discipline. As I have argued in my PhD thesis (Bengtsen 2012), we often confuse personal and disciplinary levels of thesis supervision at the university, because we think of them as different, and thus we erroneously conclude doctoral pedagogy only needs to deal with the relational and communicative dimensions of doctoral supervision practice. Though I would hold that there are reasons to keep distinguishing the two levels when reflecting analytically on doctoral pedagogy, I found in my earlier empirical research that the personal and disciplinary levels are exceedingly hard to detach in actual, specific supervision practice:

> The study concludes that a distinction between personal and disciplinary levels [of the supervisory dialogue] could make sense on an abstract level, but in the specific supervision practice I could not identify such a distinction (...). Specific supervision practice is not performed with the aim of

making separate personal and 'discipline specific' aspects, on the contrary such a form of separation seems clumsy and lacking attunement with supervision in practice. (...) From this it can be discussed whether what is traditionally described as personal [relational] recognition and sensitivity in supervision settings might rather be described as disciplinary recognition and sensitivity towards students' ways of dealing with their 'discipline specific' subject matter. (Bengtsen 2012: 182-183, my translation)

My point is here that doctoral supervision is a particularly advanced form of pedagogy because the 'disciplinary relation' between student, thesis and supervisor may change several times during the PhD. That the student requires room to find his own way through the disciplinary content influences the supervision, since the subject matter of the research project must be allowed to have a kind of 'plasticity', being moldable and elastic to different degrees depending on the particular student's stage in the process. A similar point has been made by Barnett and Coate (2006), who use the term "engaging" to point out this inextricable link between change in the research focus of the doctoral student and change in the character of the research itself. To create a disciplinary but plastic work zone for the doctoral student, supervision settings have to open up learning spaces "so that the student can develop in different ways and in her own style. A curriculum has to become (...) full of light and open spaces, different textures, shapes and relationships and arrangements for serendipitous encounters" (Barnett & Coate 2006: 129). In this context Barnett and Coate deliberately use the term "personal":

> for it is the student as a person that has to do the engaging. Whether some forms of knowledge might prompt such 'engagement' more than others, whether some pedagogies might encourage 'engagement' more than others, and whether such engagement might be understood as a form of 'construction' (...) is immaterial here. What matters ultimately is the sense of immediate personal encounter and of an individual wrestling and interlocking with the material at hand – that material, the knowledge corpus, being itself always in flux. (Barnett & Coate 2006: 61)

What is doctoral pedagogy then? How can it be understood by 'outsiders', researchers and developers, if it is so highly dependent on disciplinary insight? The important point in this section is that engaging doctoral students in their research demands motivational work from within the discipline and the student's specific research focus. It also emphasizes that supervisors should be very attentive to the specific kind of difficulty their students are facing and the specific mixture of personal and disciplinary aspects at work there. While the terms "relational pedagogy" and "student engagement" are often connected to the interpersonal realm of pedagogical work in higher education, the point here is that in doctoral supervision these terms are also very much discipline-oriented and anchored in the students' understandings of the subject matter at hand.

4.3.2 Supervising from within the discipline

The following description and discussion takes its point of departure in the aforementioned process of organizing supervision and orchestrating the supervisory dialogue (see chapters two and three). Thus, all of the four categories below are actually subcategories within the disciplinary horizon mentioned in section 4.1.2, Figure 2. This means that this section delves further into the implications of the disciplinary focus on doctoral supervision and does not simply treat it as one category among others, as is the case in the previous chapters. Based on the observations of the supervision meetings described in chapters two and three I argue that the disciplinary impact on doctoral supervision can been made visible through four main categories. These four categories together illustrate the way in which doctoral pedagogy is deeply submerged and wrapped up within a disciplinary mindset, a disciplinary discourse and, very importantly, an epistemological perspective, which does not always have clear-cut educational and pedagogical implications. The four categories that I shall present are:

- *Education*   Knowledge and skills expected to be required during a PhD
- *Discipline*   The craftsmanship, language and norms of the discipline
- *Argument*   Consistency and congruence of the overall research project
- *Subject*   The topic-specific subject matter, theories and methods

First, during the observed doctoral supervision meetings the educational dimension – the PhD courses and induction programmes in research methods – was discussed in relation to the doctoral students' research projects, in the sense of as how the newly acquired skills and knowledge would enhance the students' ability to conduct the planned research project. Some of the students as well as their supervisors expressed, during the interviews, a dissatisfaction with the present selection of PhD courses offered by the Graduate School, as these courses were felt to be not discipline-specific enough, and therefore not relevant enough to the individual doctoral student's research project. There was a tension between the desired formalized educational level of the PhD and the actual opportunities for coursework and student seminars offered by the Graduate School. In an interview with the Head of Graduate School herself, the same consideration was voiced – that the repertoire of PhD courses could be further improved, for example with more collaboration on a national level between the different universities. This points to the fact that the educational dimension of the supervision meetings was seen against the background of disciplinary relevance and depth.

Second, besides the formal educational dimension of doctoral education, the informal dimension, consisting of disciplinary lingo, norms for conducting research in specific ways and navigation within the broader research field, took up a large part of the supervisors' and students' attention during the meetings. The students' projects were continuously measured against disciplinary norms and habits of good research conduct, and the supervisors, and to a lesser degree the students, several times used canonical research studies within the discipline as role models to speak through. In this way the broader research field and horizon encompassing the individual doctoral student's research project was used as a map, containing all the different points of reference that would be relevant for situating the project in the discipline. The discipline thus functioned as the epistemological, perhaps even ontological, layout that framed the supervisory dialogue.

Third, the relationships between the different parts of the research project were also key points of reference during the supervision meetings. The consistency and progress of the project's argument occupied the supervisors and students to a large degree, and experiences of difficulties and incongruence within the research *process* were often referred to as difficulties and incongruence within the research *product*. Fourth, references to and discussions about specific research topics, theories, concepts and methods or methodologies were seen being used to address, debate and sometimes solve and other times question specific challenges within the research project. Theories, concepts and methods, were used as tools to tear down barriers within the projects, but also to build up, repair and design new research strategies. The theories, concepts and methods relevant to the individual research project constituted the epistemological syntax and semantics – the language – of the supervision taking place.

	Education	Discipline	Argument	Subject
Pedagogy embedded within:	Knowledge and skills required within discipline	Craftsmanship and language of discipline	Consistency and congruence	Topic-specific theories and methods

Figure 4

On this basis I argue that doctoral supervisors, and their students, supervise *from within* the discipline. In spite of other educational and pedagogical parameters influencing doctoral supervision, supervisors and students themselves see doctoral supervision primarily as a disciplinary event. This is visible in the agendas and topics that structure the meetings; students go to their supervisors for help first and foremost with disciplinary issues relating to challenges in the research design, interpretation of data and background theory. In the interviews with the supervisors and students, this was also present in the way they used the research project and the challenges relating to methodology and theoretical work to frame challenges in the students' learning process. Rhetorically speaking, doctoral supervisors and students put discipline before pedagogy; to put it in a more nuanced way, which is perhaps closer to the truth, doctoral supervisors and students understand and perform pedagogy *as* disciplinary work.

It can also be said that doctoral pedagogy takes place *on the inside* of the subject matter during doctoral supervision meetings. It is difficult to distinguish between a disciplinary argument and a pedagogical act. The distinction may not necessarily be relevant, but this is hard to know as researchers and developers tend to see and evaluate doctoral supervision from the outside of the discipline, and supervisors and students tend to see doctoral pedagogy from the inside. When doctoral supervisors guide or direct students they do so by activating a disciplinary framework that provides students with language, concepts, research strategies, data management processes, and other tools related to the specific research project undertaken by the student. Likewise, students having troubles managing their research and learning will typically use disciplinary language to frame the problem, posing the question as a discipline-related one, though it may not be in reality. The supervisors will in turn meet such questions with a language steeped in the terminology of the discipline and try to help the student solve the technicality, opening up the interpretation of a core concept from a new angle, reviewing the research plan and so on. This, I argue, is the working of an embedded pedagogy within doctoral supervision, which makes it tricky to speak of doctoral pedagogy without also addressing the related research issues. Conversely, the discipline-embodied nature of doctoral supervision can make it challenging for supervisors and student to assume an analytical-critical position when reflecting on their learning and teaching strategies. As the literature tells us, particularly in its numerous interview studies, there are pedagogical issues in need of further reflection and development in doctoral supervision. However, there is a lack of research into the ways pedagogical aspects attach to disciplinary vocabulary and semantics during supervision meetings.

4.3.3 The merging of pedagogy with the discipline

My argument does not serve to blame doctoral supervisors and students for lacking a vocabulary that explicates pedagogical and learning strategies. And I do not argue that doctoral supervision is empty of pedagogy. On the contrary, as I have argued elsewhere (Bengtsen 2014c; Bengtsen 2014d), doctoral supervision is full to the brim and even overflowing with pedagogy. The challenge is that there are so many forms of pedagogy taking place, and some of them, as argued here, are so deeply wrapped up in the core disciplinary semantics that it makes it very hard for outside researchers and developers to grasp fully what is going on. This means that there is an unresolved and under-researched 'tension' between discipline and pedagogy in doctoral supervision, one that is hard for researchers and developers to grasp, and, because of its typically tacit character, largely not reflected on or articulated by the supervisors and students themselves. This point leads us to question whether researchers into and developers of doctoral education should be better equipped in order to understand more fully the nature of doctoral pedagogy as an advanced form of research supervision, or whether doctoral supervisors and research programme directors, even heads of departments, should be more attuned to and engaged with generic aspects of doctoral supervision, as outlined in this book for example. The solution is probably that both things should happen more. However, neither would, in my view, solve the insider-outsider schism when researching doctoral supervision. What is needed is more collaboration across different layers of the faculty, or institution, so that the different actors within doctoral education get to know *of* each other's work, though they need not understand it completely.

Ultimately, this is a question of balance and point of view. With the increase in professionalization strategies and agendas for quality assurance at the university, one might ask if it could be said that the disciplines are wrapped up within doctoral pedagogy and educational discourses – and not the other way around. As Green points out, this question leans toward the discussion about the development of a generic doctoral curriculum (Green 2009) and a "transdisciplinary doctorate" (Willetts, Mitchell, Abeysuriya & Fam, 2012), promoted in order to ensure educational relevance for the job market and safeguard the quality of doctoral education globally. As underlined by Andres, Bengtsen, Castano, Crossouard, Keefer, and Pyhältö (Andres et al 2015), "the aim of foregrounding and developing the generic dimension of the PhD across disciplines creates tension in relation to the desire to at the same time strengthen research environments at the disciplinary level, to maintain the strong disciplinary focus of the PhD, and to resist its over-regulation (Gudmundsson 2008)" (Andres et al 2015: 15). The tendency to increase the element of 'schooling' in doctoral education raises the question of to what degree the disciplinary (local) or generic (global) elements of doctoral education are accentuated and what fundamental vision and purpose of doctoral education for the future is heeded. Personally, I see no contradictions or choices between disciplines and general pedagogical aims, but the subject will very likely be discussed intensely in the years to come.

Nevertheless, one of the future challenges for research into and development of doctoral supervision is to create more knowledge and promote more understanding of the interlocked character of discipline and pedagogy. We need to know more about what learning strategies are inscribed on the inside of doctoral students' seemingly discipline-specific questions. Such questions are certainly discipline-specific, but they may be more than that; they may hold elements of a more general doctoral pedagogy within them. One way to unearth more shades of the semantics of doctoral pedagogy could be to apply a wider range of terms and to stretch the vocabulary with which we talk about doctoral supervision learning and teaching strategies. For example, terms such as 'research supervision', 'post-graduate supervision' and 'early career researchers' cast new light on the meaning of doctoral pedagogy. 'Research supervision' enhances the focus on the research and hence also the discipline-specific elements of doctoral supervision. 'Post-graduate supervision' highlights educational elements by pointing to the connections with graduate, and even undergraduate, education. 'Early career researchers' points to the supervisor more than the student. This term sees supervision as part of the supervisors' professional development within academia. The concluding point here is that new terms could help us unlock more nuances of doctoral pedagogy, depending on where the spotlight is shone and whose perspective – the supervisors', students', or department's – it takes. So, to understand doctoral supervision more fully as an embedded pedagogy, we need to explore the different terms we use to describe this particular form of supervision, and the semantics of these terms; we also need to try for new terms to catch hold of other meanings of the discipline-embedded character of doctoral supervision.

4.4 TORN PEDAGOGY: NET-BASED DOCTORAL SUPERVISION

The final aspect of doctoral supervision as an advanced pedagogy is that of 'torn' pedagogy. This aspect in some ways encapsulates many of the previously discussed aspects, and it is highlighted in the way digital media and net-based educational technologies influence the supervision process. I argue that doctoral pedagogy is 'torn' in the sense that it may not be fruitful to see the supervision process as an holistic form of pedagogy in which all parts join neatly together to form one coherent system. We should look instead to the under-researched ways in which doctoral supervision processes are continuously torn apart, which can be clearly seen through the lens of net-based doctoral supervision.

4.4.1 A progressive view on technologies within doctoral education

Implementing and integrating educational technology at the university is today no longer a new business, and globally in doctoral education there have been "movements towards digitalisation and globalisation [and] interactivity in the learning process" (de Beer & Mason 2009: 213). However, the effect of educational technologies on doctoral supervision is still under-researched. By the turn of the millennium Price and Money (2002) stated that "[e]xtensive present-day developments in the theory and practice of mentoring have largely concentrated on close-contact mechanisms in which mentor and mentee have freedom for relatively frequent face-to-face meetings, where division of responsibility and empowerment can be facilitated and roles can be clearly defined" (Price & Money 2002: 127). Despite increasing focus on net-based doctoral education, the research undertaken during the past decade, since Price and Money's study, has not been overwhelming in scope. It tends to see educational technologies in a 'traditional' light as either enhancing peer discussion and feedback opportunities, or solving the so-called "supervisor resource problem" (de Beer & Mason 2009: 213). This traditionalist view becomes clear in de Beer and Mason's understanding of net-based doctoral supervision, and also Augustsson and Jaldemark (2014), as a means for information storage and archiving supervision meetings. This is present in their conclusion that net-based doctoral supervision is a "system where the instructions, discussions, submissions, and evaluations between supervisor and student are automatically recorded as part of the process would be far more comprehensive and complete than ad hoc summaries" (de Beer & Mason 2009: 214).

Taken from my previous work is the point that, "besides seeing net-based doctoral supervision as a support system that may enhance already known pedagogical strategies, the research in this field has also been keen to show the limitations of educational technologies. De Beer and Mason point out that the "[d]isadvantages of electronic communication include its inability to read body language cues and facial expressions; the difficulties surrounding the process of checking one's understanding of material; and the risk of critiques being too brusque or being seen by inexperienced researchers as personal criticisms" (de Beer & Mason 2009: 223). These reservations about net-based doctoral supervision are also found in Sussex (2008), who states that "[w]orking at a distance when one does not have a good personal knowledge of the other member of the supervisor-student dyad can be difficult. (...) the relationship is less evolved than that with the on-campus students, and there are channels of communication which are not present because of the lack of face-to-face contact" (Sussex 2008: 133). Even as recently as Erichsen, Bollinger and Halupa's quantitative study (2014), net-based doctoral supervision is described as more "difficult and challenging, [as] it requires more effort, focus, and commitment than traditional programs, one must also have more self-discipline, be highly organized as well as have a greater responsibility for one's self" (Erichsen, Bollinger & Halupa 2014: 330).

The face-to-face encounter has been established over the years as such a potent and important dimension of the supervisory dialogue that it has also, sometimes unintentionally, created a dichotomy between face-to-face and online contact; a hierarchy has been built in which the face-to-face relation is seen as the most primary and authentic form of contact between supervisor and student. Handal and Lauvås do not oppose net-based supervision as such, however they emphasize that the face-to-face dialogue "is not just more rich, but also attains a stronger dynamic" (Handal & Lauvås 2011: 228, my translation). As a consequence, they argue, "it is difficult to relate personally, in the good sense of the term, if you do not meet physically and talk together in that mode" (ibid., my translation). Norm Friesen, who is otherwise a promoter of online learning at university level, stresses the more immediate and flow-like qualities the face-to-face encounter possesses compared to its online counterpart. Friesen accentuates what he calls the more "crafted" aspects of online communication – one is forced to craft one's own presence explicitly and vicariously by use of digital tools (Friesen 2011: 156). According to Friesen "the offline classroom clearly appears as a place that is suitable for pedagogical practice", unlike net-based contexts that "by contrast, impose forms of specialization and classification that need to be consistently combated and counteracted by both students and teachers" (Friesen 2011: 157). Max van Manen and Catherine Adams (2009) make the same distinction between the verbal face-to-face encounter and the written dialogue by means of digital tools used for student feedback. Despite the fact that Manen and Adams are especially interested in understanding the value of presence in online writing, they give a special status to the face-to-face encounter, claiming that "the spoken word is irrevocable in a manner that is rarely true of the written word. In normal conversation or discussion, what has been said and heard cannot be taken back" (Manen & Adams 2009: 8). A hierarchy in favor of the face-to-face encounter seems to be implicitly established in research into net-based supervision; spontaneity, authenticity and interpersonal dynamics are ranked highly, and these features are more often connected to the embodied dialogue in contrast to online dialogues." (Bengtsen & Jensen 2015: 3-4).

In the following, I shall foreground a different approach to researching net-based doctoral education, in which there is a will to see it not as a rival, or otherwise in opposition, to face-to-face supervision. As pointed out in Barbara Crossouard's study (2008), as argued elsewhere in my work (Bengtsen & Jensen 2015: 16), net-based doctoral supervision can also be seen as a "differently 'windowed world', [in which the net-based] forum entailed a renegotiation of rules, divisions of labour and new identities, sometimes creating question marks around taken-for-granted subjectivities" (Crossouard 2008: 63). What is interesting in Crossouard's study is that she does not try to define a schism between net-based and face-to-face doctoral pedagogies, acknowledging that net-based forums may still establish a personal and emotional bond between supervisors and students. She argues that net-based forums may even constitute new possibilities for meeting and thus developing social relations among doctoral students. As Crossouard shows, for some students net-based forums "supported social relations that were helpful for their learning. The web site was described as 'our student bar', or a 'town hall', and gave some students a sense of belonging within the institution" (Crossouard 2008: 60). Furthermore, restating findings by Turkle, Crossouard points out that "an online environment 'gives people the chance to express multiple and often unexplored aspects of the self, to play with their identity and to try out new ones'" (Crossouard 2008: 63). From this perspective, I view educational technologies as complementary to face-to-face supervision, which opens up new possibilities but also challenges, in a constructive sense, the scope and conceptualizations of doctoral supervision practice.

A similar understanding is found in Neil Selwyn's (2013; 2014) more general description of educational technologies in the university context. Selwyn argues that we should move away from seeing educational technologies as something 'outside' and different from traditional teaching and supervision practice. Instead, Selwyn argues, universities have for a long time been steeped in technology and "[i]n reality, the majority of instances of 'digital higher education' as they have been *actually* realized and implemented are far more mundane and messy" (Selwyn 2014: 31) than is usually perceived. Furthermore, it seems that digital technologies are so deeply embedded within everyday life in higher education that it may prove difficult to study, for example, the implementation of one specific piece of software in doctoral supervision settings. Different technologies already shape supervision processes, and therefore "[a]ny changes associated with the use of digital technology in higher education are likely to be incremental, iterative and often unforeseen" (Selwyn 2014: 32). One of the most certain predictions that *can* be made of any implementation of digital technology in doctoral education is "that it is likely to involve a number of 'non-effects' as well as far-reaching unintended consequences" (ibid.). I agree with Selwyn that we need a new and more elaborate language (Selwyn 2014: 129ff.) for how digital technologies become, and are already, part of doctoral supervision practices. Such a new language, with new concepts for net-based doctoral pedagogy, will enable researchers and developers to move beyond the schism between face-to-face and net-based forums for doctoral supervision. Such a change in approach, I argue, will move the focus away from the digital technologies themselves and towards new forms of doctoral pedagogy that are disclosed through the analysis of net-based doctoral supervision.

4.4.2 Net-based doctoral supervision as a 'torn' pedagogy

What I shall present here is not the use of one specific digital tool during the observed supervision meetings, but the more general presence of digital technology in the doctoral supervision processes. It is striking that the net-based technologies supported each of the supervision meetings tacitly and implicitly, in an almost 'embodied' manner, meaning as being *part of* the supervision action and process, and not outside it. In all the supervision meetings I observed there had been communication before the meeting, for example students would typically have sent material to the supervisor to comment on. In some instances the supervisors had already provided some comments or remarks on the material even before the meeting took place. In others there had been a correspondence about the agenda for the meeting, and some supervisors would send their students reminders about things to put on the agenda shortly before the session took place. During some of the meetings computers and tablets were used to illustrate points with figures or diagrams; to browse for relevant references; to look up specific issues concerning rules and regulation for the PhD; to check guidelines for thesis submission and the PhD defense; to revisit information about an upcoming conference for which the student is submitting a paper; to look up possible networking opportunities for a research stay abroad; and finally to write emails to other researchers to clarify disciplinary issues, or to heads of departments and the graduate school to ask questions about the framework of the PhD process at the specific department or institute.

This finding is interesting because supervisors and students do not consciously reflect on these integrations of net-based technologies into their supervision meetings. They simply seem to take them for granted. This reaches back to Selwyn's important point that in order to understand the influence of digital technologies on higher education practice – doctoral education in this context – we should look beyond so-called new technologies that arise and interrupt our daily practice. We should also look at the more mundane, but important, dealings we have with net-based technologies in our everyday practice. Net-based technologies in doctoral education can be said to be ubiquitous (Selwyn 2013; Dalsgaard, Pedersen & Aaen 2013) in the sense that they saturate doctoral supervision practice and have done so for some time now, but on a relatively tacit and implicit level, which is nevertheless of great importance to the organizational and pedagogical aspects of doctoral supervision. Where Crossouard (2008) speaks of net-based technologies as constituting a "town hall" or "student bar", I shall argue that they constitute an archipelago of different digital tools and services that might be said to manifest a culture or civilization in themselves. My point is that even though the digital tools are implicitly experienced as servants or handmaids by doctoral supervisors and students, they also constitute a force in themselves. They should more properly be seen as independent forces that may be working with them or against them depending on whether they are successfully integrated into the supervision processes or not. When a server breaks down, an email fails to send or files are hacked or deleted, the tacit force of such technologies become present.

This leads to my argument that net-based technologies constitute a 'torn' element within doctoral pedagogy (the term 'torn' was originally coined in Bengtsen & Mathiasen 2014). They reveal themselves as such when they 'break' or do not work according to the expected function, disrupting the meeting, even if only momentarily. This is seen, for example, when supervisors and students spend a good deal of time discussing which file is the most recent version of the student's work, or when the student sends the supervisor a specific piece of information (or vice-versa) that is needed in the meeting but has never arrived because the mailbox has reached its storage quota. This is one way that net-based technologies may 'tear' the supervision meeting and create dissonance. Another piece of supporting evidence may be found in the fact that all the communication taking place by means of net-based technologies before, during and after the face-to-face meeting demonstrates that the meeting is not the all-powerful nexus of contact and research innovation that more traditionalist research into the nature of net-based doctoral supervision sees it as. In actuality, doctoral supervision is *not* ultimately tied down to the face-to-face encounter, just as the doctoral students' work spaces are not tied down to particular physical places on campus. This finding disrupts the traditional 'heliocentric', or holistic, understanding of doctoral supervision as taking place in a series of face-to-face encounters where the processes occurring between the meetings are dealt with. This is not the case. During the observed meetings it became clear that supervisors and students communicate continuously about all sorts of issues, whether in face-to-face supervision meetings, informal ad hoc meetings in the hallway or during the lunch break and so on.

Doctoral supervision does not consist of neatly demarcated areas or dialogue units in face-to-face meetings and email correspondences, but is instead scattered through and across the PhD process. As was observed during meetings, supervisors and students could conduct a face-to-face dialogue and an email correspondence with each other, or other relevant people, at the same time – just as in some meetings they spent a good deal of the face-to-face dialogue in concluding an email correspondence begun a month ago. In some instances, then, face-to-face meetings functioned as commentary on a previous net-based dialogue, and not the other way around.

In addition, bits and pieces of dialogue from earlier net-based correspondence would suddenly pop up during face-to-face meetings and redirect the conversation by evoking an exchange of text material and feedback dating back several weeks, or sometimes months. In this way net-based technologies make visible the torn character of doctoral supervision. This is not meant negatively, but it acknowledges that doctoral supervision is a kaleidoscopic and fragmented event, not broken or destroyed by the disruptions of net-based technologies, but attaining a form of cohesion, flow and flexibility often ignored or overlooked by supervisors and students themselves through the deeply tacit nature of the 'old' net-based technologies used in doctoral supervision settings.

4.4.3 Torn doctoral pedagogy enhances flexibility and criticality

Net-based doctoral supervision makes visible a central aspect of the advanced nature of doctoral pedagogy. During the PhD supervisors and students communicate a lot, by different means and in different contexts. This sprawling form of communication sometimes assumes a life of its own, slipping from the grasp of the supervisors and students. Elsewhere in my work I have described how net-based teaching and supervision in higher education can be viewed as a form of 'guerrilla' pedagogy and described with the "concept of 'guerrilla' didactics' to point out that IT-educational didactics can never be viewed from above or beyond the different digital platforms used, but must be planned, re-planned, broken up and displaced in order to remerge as a dynamic and plastic pulse through different contexts as they change during the course" (Bengtsen, Mathiasen & Dalsgaard 2015: 123). Thus, doctoral supervision is constantly on the move, repeatedly assuming new forms and addressing and readdressing deeply entangled issues not only in the students' research projects, but also in the the many levels of PhD education itself. This gives doctoral supervisors and students opportunities to keep in touch, to inform each other of relevant comments and amendments to the research and to give different forms of feedback in the periods when they do not meet face-to-face, but also to keep the research project and scientific horizon plastic and flexible.

I argue that disclosing doctoral supervision as a torn pedagogy actually does not entail a point about increasing complexity in doctoral education. On the contrary, the effect net-based technologies were observed to have on doctoral supervision meetings, and more generally on the PhD – as became clear during the interviews with the supervisors and students – brought forth an understanding of a new form of cohesion, flow and flexibility in the supervision process. The ongoing dialogues taking place through net-based technologies seemed to enhance the outcome of the face-to-face meetings for supervisors as well as students, since the meetings, in this light, were more continuations of an ongoing dialogue than initiations of new dialogues. This flow of the dialogue seemed to follow the research process more closely as it progressed, as opposed to retrospectively treating it at face-to-face meetings with no, or little, contact between meetings. I argue that this form of supervision has a flexibility that is not seen in supervision settings where the face-to-face meetings are the sole platform for dialogue. There are simply more possibilities for doctoral supervisors and students to participate in and comment on each other's feedback, questions and thought processes generally.

Furthermore, I argue that the diverse feedback systems of net-based doctoral supervision enhance capacity for criticism in doctoral students' learning processes. The diverse nature of the feedback doctoral students receive from their peers, as shown in Crossouard (2008) and Bengtsen, Mathiasen and Dalsgaard (2015), enhances their ability to criticize their own work. This links to earlier points made about the variation and complexity in dialogues in doctoral supervision meetings, which are increased through the use of net-based technologies. This makes possible different forms of thinking that might not otherwise have been encouraged by simple face-to-face contact between students and between students and their supervisors. Net-based technologies influence the way supervisors and students think together as they "play against each other and strike back at us [teachers and supervisors] with voices of their own" (Bengtsen, Mathiasen & Dalsgaard 2015: 125; see also: Bengtsen & Mathiasen 2014; Bengtsen & Jensen 2015). Using net-based technologies demands that both doctoral supervisors and students develop extra awareness of their communication styles, as well as an awareness of whether the particular digital tool is suitable for and supportive of the form of dialogue they wish to have. Torn pedagogy makes the supervision space itself flexible, but it also requires doctoral supervisors to develop sensitivity to a greater variation and diversity in forms of contact, and perhaps also forms of thinking, than in traditional face-to-face-only settings.

4.5 CONCLUSION

Based on the findings and discussions in chapters two and three, five core pedagogical dimensions have been unearthed and used to characterize doctoral supervision as an advanced pedagogy. These five core structural elements within doctoral pedagogy have been shown to mark out doctoral supervision's core qualities in terms of the form of pedagogy that emerges against the backdrop of the unique organizational, dialogical, curricular and disciplinary conditions that constitute doctoral supervision practice. It has been argued that doctoral supervision is constituted as:

an **ambivalent** pedagogy, because of the fundamental push-pull mechanism in the supervisors' double formational and educational performances – both teaching the students (pulling them in) and facilitating their emancipatory development (pushing them away). What was of particular interest in my own study was that this push-pull relation does not take place merely on a personal-academic emancipatory level, but also on a epistemological level, which relates to the nature of the doctoral student's *thinking*.

a **subtle** pedagogy, because of the multi-layered and multi-pedagogical character of doctoral supervision meetings. Doctoral supervision does not consist of one single core unit with annexed contexts, but of several educational 'folds', no single one of which can be said to be primary during the meetings. This means that not one but several pedagogies constitute the nature of doctoral supervision practice.

an **idiosyncratic** pedagogy, because during the meetings doctoral supervisors and students withdraw into their own thought-spaces and critically reflect on the substance of the dialogue within their own internal systems of reference; it is not always possible to connect these systems to the joint dialogue. However, the important point in this study is that this is not something that should be solved, amended or avoided, but an essential catalyst of the supervisory dialogue.

an **embedded** pedagogy, because the pedagogy of doctoral supervision is deeply entrenched in the disciplinary and curricular framework of the PhD. This is visible in the way that doctoral supervisors and students tacitly link challenges in learning and teaching to questions about how to deal with disciplinary and curricular elements. The central point here is that in order to understand the nature of doctoral supervision fully, this embedded nature of doctoral pedagogy must be explored further and cast in a more context-relevant pedagogical vocabulary.

a **torn** pedagogy, because of its gradual, but inescapable and increasing, entanglement with a variety of net-based technologies that give the communication between supervisors and students a fragmented and kaleidoscopic character. However, this does not mean that net-based doctoral supervision threatens core issues of trust, professional intimacy and deep and active listening. Furthermore, I argue that net-based technologies can enhance valued elements such as criticality, process focus, ongoing contact, cohesion and flow in the supervision process.

These five core structural elements constitute doctoral pedagogy as an advanced pedagogy. Though all of them may be said to be part of every pedagogy within higher education, I propose that they are particular to doctoral education because of the scope and weight of the organizational and dialogical dimensions from which they arise. Having been extracted from the conditions of doctoral supervision laid bare in chapters two and three, these five elements are generic constituents of a *doctoral* pedagogy. They are generic in the sense that they emerged as core constituents from the observations and interviews conducted in this study. This does not mean that they are universal; nor does it mean that they are absolute in the sense that no other supplementary constituting elements may be discovered. It is certain, for instance, that different national contexts have their own particular constituents for a doctoral pedagogy (Andres et al 2015). However, I argue that these five constituents, when viewed against the international research literature within the field, as has been done throughout his book, appear to be generic in a sense that makes them relevant for discussion and reflection in a wider international context.

My conclusion that the five constituents reveal doctoral education to be an advanced pedagogy does not mean that other forms of pedagogy, say in early childhood education, primary or secondary schools, are not just as advanced in their own way. In this respect, any educational context holds the potential for working out an advanced pedagogy of its own. With the term 'advanced' I argue that doctoral supervision should acknowledge two things. First, that it *does* have its own kind of pedagogy due to the particular organizational, relational and disciplinary aspects and conditions shown in chapters two and three. This is an invitation – perhaps a polemical one – for researchers and developers within doctoral education to raise their ambitions in working out a pedagogy that matches the complexity, subtlety and idiosyncrasy of doctoral supervision. Second, the term 'advanced' signals to supervisors, students, directors of graduate studies, heads of departments and deans, that there *is* a thing called doctoral pedagogy, and it must be taken into account by all the mentioned parties in order to enhance the levels of student satisfaction, learning outcomes and research contributions of the PhD.

PART 5

CODA: FUTURE APPROACHES TO DOCTORAL SUPERVISION

In conclusion, I wish to draw attention to some overlooked and under-researched dimensions of doctoral education that need to be studied more closely in order to develop not only the research field, but also doctoral educational practice itself. There are three issues in particular that are in acute need of research: (1) strong thinking; (2) terminology; and (3) advanced pedagogy. I do not intend to replace or criticize more traditional approaches within doctoral education research, but to contribute with more nuances to certain issues, and to shed light on poorly lit spaces.

5.0 STRONG THINKING

First, I suggest a move from the traditional understanding of relations in doctoral supervision as emotional and social aspects of pedagogy to an understanding of *thinking* as the core relational dimension. Doctoral supervisors and students build strong relations of trust, honesty and respect through their mutual engagement in the *thinking* process. This calls for further research into what I have referred to as the epistemological sides of doctoral pedagogy – how supervisors and students think together and conceive of the research project and its challenges and potentials, and the different approaches they have to wielding, creating and managing concepts. In this context thinking should *not* be understood as a nostalgic longing for more idealistic or cognitive forms of pedagogy that have been lost in contemporary doctoral education. Instead, thinking should be viewed as firmly grounded in the research topics and processes of the doctoral students' work, and deeply anchored within the organizational infrastructure, in its formal, informal and non-formal manifestations in the departmental and institutional environments that surround doctoral work in universities today. It should also be stressed that thinking within doctoral supervision is defined by its uniquely relational character, which marks out the substance of doctoral pedagogy. Thinking takes on a dialogical form that weaves the disciplinary, organizational and personal dimensions of doctoral research supervision together.

Secondly, it cannot be emphasized enough that doctoral pedagogy 'matters' in the sense that it is deeply subject matter-oriented. Doctoral supervisors and students are certainly concerned with learning and teaching strategies, but they see their task primarily as one of making a thorough, consistent, robust and original contribution to the field, and to unlock new understandings of the subject matter in hand. Global drivers in doctoral education, educational politics and transferable skills relevant for the future work force are all very important issues for the professionalized university, and they have all received a great deal of attention in work within doctoral education in recent years – in many ways rightfully so. However, we must acknowledge that at the level of research supervision itself, the level of doctoral supervisors and students, the world is seen from *within* the disciplinary perspective. The force and creativity of doctoral pedagogy comes first and foremost from an *obsession* with the subject matter and disciplinary significance of the individual doctoral student's research project. As such, doctoral supervision should be researched not only as an accumulation of support systems, learning approaches and feedback strategies, but as a form of pedagogical alchemy that transforms the fibers of the subject matter itself.

This should not be seen as a reactive approach to research and development within doctoral education, as it builds on the professionalization and quality assurance paradigm of policy today. Rather, it should be seen as a complementary approach that anchors research into doctoral supervision within the subject matter and acknowledges that the unique pedagogical features of research supervision are ultimately about doing research. This is not to say that persons come second, or that identity formation within doctoral education is not relevant. My aim is to focus on the inextricable link between, and the interweaving of, persons and subject matter that lies at the heart of doctoral pedagogy. Doctoral supervision *is* about students finding their own voices, but it is not so much about finding voices as researchers generally; it seems more important for doctoral supervisors to support doctoral students in finding their own voices as future historians, philosophers, linguists, archaeologists, etc., which is really about the great diversity and pluralism inherent within doctoral education.

5.1 TERMINOLOGY

Future research into doctoral supervision and education could take advantage of the differences in the terminology and semantics in discourses about doctoral pedagogy. The current confusion in terminology leads to blurred arguments, when terms such as 'research supervision', 'doctoral supervision', 'postgraduate supervision' and 'early career research' are used interchangeably. I am not arguing for a homogenous and 'totalitarian' terminology in which each term can mean only one specific thing. Instead I argue that the different terms and their semantics could be further explored and made use of in order to strengthen cohesion within the research field, and focus more sharply on precisely which dimensions of doctoral education are being dealt with. I think there is potential for developing pedagogies around these different terms. 'Research supervision', for example, could invite for studies into research-intensive pedagogies revolving around the intellectual and epistemological aspects of doctoral education – whereas, for example, 'postgraduate supervision' could denote a focus on the inherent pedagogical aspects of formalization of, and student environments within, doctoral education.

This is not to say that a more holistic view on doctoral education is not useful, and at the end of the day it should come together for the individual student as one coherent educational whole. However, we should aim at more depth and precision in the vocabulary we use to talk about doctoral pedagogies. This also points back to the terminology issue itself – that doctoral education has a molten core semantically speaking, since it is still a relatively young field of research that is being explored through all kinds of different approaches. However, despite the fact that research into doctoral education has been happening for quite a few decades now, the field sometimes finds itself on a slippery footing, and the different traditions and discourses are still rather messily tossed together in vaguely titled journals and conferences that cover the entire field but might benefit from a more focused approach. In sum: I am actually arguing that doctoral education as a field of research has reached a level of maturity where it makes sense to subdivide different discourses, research approaches and educational foci more systematically in order to use the many-sidedness of the phenomenon to achieve greater precision and robustness in the research in the years to come.

5.3 ADVANCED PEDAGOGY

This book has critically reflected upon, but also acknowledged, the advanced form of pedagogy at work in doctoral supervision settings, and it is impressive to see the ways supervisors and also students, engage in this complex and potent learning space that works on so many different educational levels at the same time. As mentioned earlier, the term 'advanced' does not mean that doctoral pedagogy is a finer or necessarily more sophisticated form of pedagogy than other forms of education, whether in schools, colleges or vocational environments. I use it instead to mean that when you turn doctoral supervision inside out, as I have attempted to do, you can see the many organizational layers simultaneously at work and the subtle forms of navigation demanded of supervisors and students in the multiple and interrelated dimensions of the PhD. It is also interesting to witness the different pedagogies, which all in their own ways try to facilitate the demanding learning curve that is meant to take students from initiates in their field to stewards of the discipline (Golde & Walker 2006; Walker et al 2008). There lies a heavy responsibility on both supervisors and students to approach that task in as constructive a manner as possible during the PhD. There are always disciplinary, organizational and personal aspects in play which must be balanced, supported and critiqued in subtle and complex ways during the process.

The literature on doctoral education has a tendency to focus on management issues – it is more about how to control and structure the PhD, and not so much about the importance of supervisors making themselves vulnerable in the sense of exposing their own ways of managing *their* research, and how *they* think. The importance of doctoral supervisors being able to *think with* students links back to my argument about thinking and dialogue above, but here I wish to stress a different point. This is not a repetition of the well-known apprenticeship model in which the supervisor through her function as a role model lets the student work beside her as an assistant in her own work. I wish here to reprise the idea of supervising *with* students. In this mode supervisors do not take on the student's perspective, or force their own perspective on the student, but in a constructive and open manner they explore the ideas, challenges and structures of the student's research processes. They let the student inside their own thinking processes and habits of mind (Halse & Malfroy 2010) while at the same time being aware that it is not their project but the student's, and that they are working more as a companion – not a partner or a colleague, and not a parent, but a companion. The 'companion' is a helpful role description as it positions doctoral supervisors as a central source of support and critical feedback, without overshadowing the research process. A 'companion' is not quite as vital as a 'partner' or a 'parent', and the word has a touch of a more instrumental meaning to it that could indicate how supervisors help doctoral students find their own balance and voice. Doctoral supervision should thus be seen as something to be used, and used up, perhaps even discarded if the resources are properly exhausted. To let oneself be used, but not misused, affords an instrumental meaning to the supervisor's role, to the advantage of supervisors and students alike.

REFERENCES

Acker, S., Hill, T. & Black, E. (1994). Thesis supervision in the social sciences: managed or negotiated? In *Higher Education*, Vol. 28, pp.483-498

Andres, L., Bengtsen, S., Crossouard, B., Gallego, L., Keefer, J., & Pyhältö, K. (2015). Drivers and Interpretations of Doctoral Education Today: National Comparisons. *Frontline Learning Research*. Vol. 3, No. 2, pp. 63-80

Armitage, A. (2008). Power relationships and postgraduate supervision. *Journal of Quality, Chartered Quality Institute*, December Issue

Augustsson, G. & Jaldemark, J. (2014). Online supervision: a theory of supervisors' strategic communicative influence on student dissertations. *Higher Education*. Vol. 67, pp.19-33

Bargar, R. & Duncan, J. (1982). Cultivating Creative Endeavor in Doctoral Research. *The Journal of Higher Education*. Vol.53, No.1, pp.1-31

Barnett, R. (2015a). The Time of Reason and the Ecological University. In Gibbs, P., Oili-Helena, Y., Guzmán-Valenzuela, C., & Barnett, R. (Eds.). *Universities in the Flux of Time. An exploration of time and temporality in university life*. London & New York: Routledge

Barnett, R. (2015b). *Thinking and Rethinking the University. The selected works of Ronald Barnett*. London & New York: Routledge

Barnett, R. (2007). *A Will To Learn. Being a Student in an Age of Uncertainty*. Berkshire: Open University Press

Barnett, R. & Coate, K. (2006). *Engaging the Curriculum in Higher Education*. Berkshire: Open University Press

Bartlett, A. & Mercer, G. (Eds.) (2001a). *Postgraduate Research Supervision. Transforming (R)Elations*. New York: Peter Lang

Bartlett, A. & Mercer, G. (2001b). Mostly Metaphors: Theorizing from a Practice of Supervision. In Bartlett, A. & Mercer, G. (Eds.). *Postgraduate Research Supervision. Transforming (R) Elations*. New York: Peter Lang

Batchelor, D. (2014). Finding a Voice as a Student. In Gibbs, P. & Barnett, R. (Eds.). *Thinking about Higher Education*. Springer International Publishing

Batchelor, D. (2008). Have students got a voice? In Barnett, R. & Di Napoli, R. (Eds.). *Changing Identities in Higher Education. Voicing Perspectives*. (pp.40-54). London & New York: Routledge

Batchelor, D. (2006). Vulnerable Voices: An examination of the concept of vulnerability in relation to student voice. IN: *Educational Philosophy and Theory*. Vol. 38, No. 6, pp.787-800

Becher, T. & Trowler, P.R. (2001). *Academic Tribes and Territories*. Buckingham: The Open University Press

Bengtsen, S. (2014a). *Review of the handbook literature on doctoral supervision.* Published on the website of the Graduate School, Faculty of Arts, Aarhus University: http://phd. au.dk/fileadmin/grads.au.dk/AR/ Review_doctoral_supervision.pdf

Bengtsen, S. (2014b). Position Paper for the EARLI-SIG Inaugural Meeting on Doctoral Education 21-23. September, at the Faculty of Psychology, Educational and Sport Sciencies. Blanquerna. Universitat Ramon Llull, Barcelona.

Bengtsen, S. (2014c). Dannelse i overflod. Om universitetspædagogikkens luksusproblem. In Tanggaard, L., Rømer, T.A., & Brinkmann, S. (Eds.). *Uren Pædagogik 2*. Aarhus: Klim

Bengtsen, S. (2014d). Into the Heart of Things. Defrosting Educational Theory. In Gibbs, P. & Barnett, R. (Eds.). *Thinking about Higher Education*. Springer Publishing

Bengtsen, S. (2013). Dannelsens korridor. Et argument for et udvidet dannelsesbegreb. In Pahuus, M. (Ed.). *Dannelse i en læringstid*. Aalborg: Aalborg University Press

Bengtsen, S. (2012). *Didactics and idiosyncrasy. A study of the relation between personality and professionalism in supervision meetings at the university.* PhD.-thesis. The Faculty of Arts, Aarhus University, Denmark.

Bengtsen, S. (2011). Getting personal – what does it mean? A critical discussion of the personal dimension of thesis supervision in higher education. In *London Review of Education*, Vol. 9,No. 1, March issue 2011(pp.109-118)

Bengtsen, S. & Barnett, R. (2015 – forthcoming). Confronting the Dark Side of Higher Education. *Journal of Philosophy of Education.*

Bengtsen, S., Mathiasen, H. & Dalsgaard, C. (2015). Net-based guerrilla didactics. In Fossland, T., Mathiasen, H. & Solberg, M. (Eds.). *Academic Bildung in Net-based Higher Education. Moving beyond learning* (pp.105-127). London & New York: Routledge

Bengtsen, S. & Jensen, G. (2015). Online supervision at the university. A comparative study of supervision on student assignments face-to-face and online. In *Læring & Medier (LOM)*, No.13, 2015, ISSN: 1903-248X, pp.1-23

Bengtsen, S. & Mathiasen, H. (2014). Researching online supervision. The need for a 'torn' methodology. In *Academic Quarter*. Vol. 9, pp.198-210

Bengtsen, S. & Nørgård, R.T. (2014). *Becoming jelly: a call for gelatinous pedagogy within higher education.* Proceedings of the 9th International Conference on Networked Learning 2014. Edited by Bayne, S., Jones, C., de Laat, M., Ryberg, T., & Sinclair, C. ISBN 978-1-86220-304-4

Biesta, G.J.J. (2006). *Beyond Learning. Democratic Education for a Human Future*. Boulder & London: Paradigm Publishers

Brew, A. & Peseta, T. (2009). Changing postgraduate supervision practice: a programme to encourage learning through reflection and feedback. *Innovations in Education and Teaching International*. Vol. 41, No. 1, pp.5-22

Brodin, E. (2014). Critical and creative thinking nexus: learning experiences of doctoral students. *Studies in Higher Education*, 2014. DOI: 10.1080/03075079.2014.943656

Brown, G. & Atkins, M. (1988). *Effective Teaching in Higher Education*. London: Routledge

Boud, D. & Lee, A. (Eds.) (2009). *Changing Practices of Doctoral Education*. London & New York: Routledge

Boud, D. & Lee, A. (2005). 'Peer learning' as pedagogic discourse for research education. *Studies in Higher Education*. Vol. 30, No. 5, pp.501-516

Bowen, W.G. & Rudenstein, N.L. (1992). *In Pursuit of the PhD*. Princeton, New Jersey: Princeton University Press

Brearley, L. & Hamm, T. (2013). Spaces between indigenous and nonindigenous knowledge systems (pp.259-278). IN Engels-Schwarzpaul, A.-Chr. & Peters, M.A. *Of Other Thoughts: Non-Traditional Ways to the Doctorate. A Guidebook for Candidates and Supervisors*. Rotterdam: Sense Publishers

Buber, M. (2013). *I and Thou*. Translated by Ronald G. Smith. London & New York: Bloomsbury Academic

Burnett, P. (1999). The Supervision of Doctoral Dissertations Using a Collaborative Cohort Model. *Counselor Education and Supervision*. Vol.39, September 1999, pp.46-52

Carter, S. (2014). Responding to cross-campus student requirements. In Carter, S. & Laurs, D. (Eds.). *Developing Generic Support for Doctoral Students. Practice and Pedagogy*. London & New York: Routledge

Carter, S. & Laurs, D. (Eds.) (2014). *Developing Generic Support for Doctoral Students. Practice and Pedagogy*. London & New York: Routledge

Cherry, N. (2012). The paradox and fog of supervision. Site for the encounters and growth of praxis, persons and voices. *Quality Assurance in Education*. Vol. 20, No. 1, pp.6-19

Cotterall, S. (2013). More than just a brain: emotions and the doctoral experience. *Higher Education Research & Development*. Vol. 32, No. 2, 174-187

Cottrell, S. (2014). *Dissertations and Project Reports. A Step by Step Guide*. New York: Palgrave Macmillan

Crossouard, B. (2008). Developing alternative models of doctoral supervision with online formative assessment. *Studies in Continuing Education*. Vol. 30, No. 1, pp.51-67

Cryer, P. (2006). *The Research Student's Guide to Success*. Berkshire: Open University Press

Dalsgaard, C., Pedersen, N.F. & Aaen, J. (2013). Læring på tværs af kontekster – læringspotentialer i mobilt medieret information og kommunikation. *Læring & Medier (LOM)*, Vol. 10, pp.1-23

Danby, S. & Lee, A. (2012). Framing doctoral pedagogy as design and action. In Lee, A. & Danby, S. (Eds.). *Reshaping Doctoral Education. International approaches and pedagogies*. London & New York: Routledge

De Beer, M. & Mason, R.B. (2009). Using a blended learning approach to facilitate postgraduate supervision. *Innovations in Education and*

Teaching International. Vol. 46, No. 2, pp.213-226

Delamont, S., Atkinson, P. & Parry, O. (2004). *Supervising the Doctorate. A Guide to Success.* Berkshire: The Open University Press

Delamont, S., Atkinson, P. & Parry, O. (2000). *The Doctoral Experience. Success and Failure in Graduate School.* London & New York: Falmer Press

Deleuze, G. (2006). *The Fold.* London & New York: Continuum

Doloriert, C., Sambrook, S. & Stewart, J. (2012). Power and emotion in doctoral supervision: implications for HRD. *European Journal of Training and Development.* Vol. 36, No. 7, pp.732-750

Dysthe, O. & Samara, A. (Eds.). Forskningsveiledning på Master- og Doktorgradsnivå. Oslo: Abstrakt Forlag

Dysthe, O., Samara, A., & Westrheim, K. (2006). Multivoiced supervision of Master's students: a case study of alternative supervision practices in higher education. *Studies in Higher Education,* 31 (3), pp.299-318

Eley, A. & Murray, R. (2009). *How to be an Effective Supervisor.* Berkshire: McGraw Hill, The Open University Press

Eley, A.R. & Jennings, R. (2005). *Effective Postgraduate Supervision. Improving the Student/Supervisor Relationship.* Berkshire: The Open University Press

Elliot, D.L., Reid, K., & Baumfield, V. (2015). Beyond the amusement, puzzlement and challenges: an enquiry into international students' academic acculturation. *Studies in Higher Education.* DOI: 10.1080/03075079.2015.1029903

Engels-Schwarzpaul, A.-Chr. & Peters, M.A. (2013). *Of Other Thoughts: Non-Traditional Ways to the Doctorate. A Guidebook for Candidates and Supervisors.* Rotterdam: Sense Publishers

Epstein, D., Boden, R. & Kenway, J. (2005). *Teaching and supervision.* Sage Publications

Erichsen, A.E., Bollinger, D.U., & Halupa, C. (2014). Student satisfaction with graduate supervision in doctoral programs primarily delivered in distance education settings. *Studies in Higher Education.* Vol. 39, No. 2, pp.321-338

Friesen, N. (2011). *The Place of the Classroom and the Space of the Screen. Relational Pedagogy and Internet Technology.* New York: Peter Lang

Gardner, S.K. & Mendoza, P. (Eds.) (2010). *On Becoming a Scholar. Socialization and Development in Doctoral Education.* Sterling: Stylus Publishing

Gatfield, T.J. (2005). An investigation into PhD supervisory management styles: Development of a dynamic conceptual model and its managerial implications. *Journal of Higher Education Policy and Management.* 27.3: 311-325

Gibbs, P. & Barnett, R. (Eds.). *Thinking about Higher Education.* Springer International Publishing

Godskesen, M. & Wichmann-Hansen, G. (2013). Aktiv lytning i ph.d.-vejledning – et værktøj til udvikling af dialogiske kompetencer. *Dansk Universitetspædagogisk Tidsskrift.* Vol. 8, No. 15, pp.145-157

Golde, C.M. (2010). Entering Different Worlds. Socialization Into Disciplinary Communities. In Gardner, S.K. & Mendoza, P. (Eds.). *On Becoming a Scholar. Socialization and Development in Doctoral Education*. Sterling, Virginia: Stylus Publishing

Golde, C.M. & Walker, G.E. (Eds.) (2006). *Envisioning the Future of Doctoral Education. Preparing Stewarts of the Discipline*. San Francisco: Jossey-Bass

Grant, B.M. (2010). Improvising together. The play of dialogue in humanities supervision. *Arts and Humanities in Higher Education*. Vol. 9 (3), pp.271-288

Grant, B.M. (2008). Agonistic struggle master-slave dialogues in humanities supervision. *Arts and Humanities in Higher Education*, 7(1), 9-27

Grant, B.M. (2005). Fighting for space in supervision: fantasies, fairytales, fictions and fallacies. *International Journal of Qualitative Studies in Education*. Vol. 18, No. 3, pp.337-354

Grant, B.M. (2003). Mapping the pleasures and risks of supervision discourse. *Studies in the Cultural Politics of Education*, 24(2), 176-189

Grant, B.M. (2001). Dirty Work: "A Code for Supervision" Read Against the Grain. In Bartlett, A. & Mercer, G (Eds.). *Postgraduate Research Supervision. Transforming (R)Elations*. New York: Peter Lang

Grant, B.M. (1999). Walking on a rackety bridge: mapping supervision. Paper for the HERDSA Annual International Conference, Melbourne, 12-15 July 1999

Green, B. (2009). Challenging perspectives, challenging practices. Doctoral education in transition. In Boud, D. & Lee, A. (Eds). *Changing Practices of Doctoral Education*. London & New York: Routledge

Green, B. (2005). Unfinished business: subjectivity and supervision. *Higher Education Research & Development*. Vol. 24, No. 2, pp.151-163

Green, H. & Powell, S. (2005). *Doctoral Study in Contemporary Higher Education*. Berkshire: Open University Press

Gudmundsson, H.K. (2008). Nordic Countries. In Nerad, M., & Heggelund, M. (Eds.). *Toward a Global PhD? Forces & Forms in Doctoral Education Worldwide*. Seattle & London: University of Washington Press

Gurr, G.M. (2001). Negotiating the "Rackety Bridge" – a Dynamic Model for Aligning Supervisory Style with Research Student Development. *Higher Education Research & Development*. Vol. 20, No. 1, pp.81-92

Halse, C. (2011). 'Becoming a supervisor': the impact of doctoral supervision on supervisor's learning. *Studies in Higher Education*. Vol. 36, No. 5, pp. 557-570

Halse, C. & Bansel, P. (2012). The learning alliance: ethics in doctoral supervision. *Oxford Review of Education*. Vol. 38, No. 4, pp.377-392

Halse, C. & Malfroy, J. (2010). Retheorizing doctoral supervision as professional work. *Studies in Higher Education*. Vol. 35, No. 1, pp.79-92

Handal, G. & Lauvås, P. (2011). *Forskningsveilederen*. Oslo: Cappelen, Akademisk Forlag

Hansen, F.T. (2011). Den taktfulde vejleder – om at forblive ved vejledningens sag. In Plant, P., Nielsen, G.F.

& Hansen, F.T. (Eds.). *Vejledningsdidaktik*. Albertslund: Schultz

Hansen, F.T. (2010). The Phenomenology of Wonder in Higher Education. In Brinkmann, M. (Ed.). *Erziehung. Phänomenologische Perspektiven.* (pp.161-177). Würzburg: Königshausen & Neumann

Hansen, F.T. (2008). *At stå i det åbne. Dannelse gennem filosofisk undren og nærvær.* København: Hans Reitzels Forlag

Harman, G. (2005). *Guerilla Metaphysics. Phenomenology and the Carpentry of Things.* Chicago: Open Court

Hockey, J. (1997). A complex craft: United Kingdom PhD supervision in the social sciences. *Research in Post-Compulsory Education.* Vol.2, No.1, pp.45-70

Hockey, J. (1996). A contractual solution to problems in the supervision of PhD degrees in the UK. *Studies in Higher Education.* Vol. 21, No. 3, pp. 359-371

Jazvac-Martek, M., Chen, S., & McAlpine, L. (2011). Tracking the Doctoral Student Experience over Time: Cultivating Agency in Diverse Spaces. IN McAlpine & Amundsen (Eds.). *Doctoral Education: Researched-Based Strategies for Doctoral Students, Supervisors and Administrators.* Springer Publishing

Johnson, L., Lee, A. & Green, B. (2000). The PhD and the Autonomous Self: gender, rationality and postgraduate pedagogy. *Studies in Higher Education.* Vol. 25, No. 2, pp. 135-147

Katz, J. & Hartnett, R.T. (1976). *Scholars in the Making. The Development of Graduate and Professional Students.* Cambridge, Massachusetts: Ballinger Publishing Company

Kearns, H., Gardiner, M., & Marshall, K. (2008). Innovation in PhD completion: the hardy shall succeed (and be happy!). *Higher Education Research & Development*, Vol. 27, No. 1, pp.77-89

Kiley, M. (2009). Identifying threshold concepts and proposing strategies to support doctoral candidates. *Innovations in Education and Teaching International.* Vol.46, No.3, pp.293-304

Kiley, M. & Wisker, G. (2009). Threhold concepts in research education and evidence of threshold crossing. *Higher Education Research & Development.* Vol.28, No.4, August 2009, pp.431-441

Kobayashi, S., Grout, B., & Rump, C. (2013). Interaction and learning in PhD supervision – a qualitative study of supervision with multiple supervisors. IN *Dansk Universitetspædagogisk Tidsskrift.* Årgang 8, Nr. 14, pp.13-25

Land, R. (2008). Academic development. Identity and paradox. In Barnett, R. & Di Napoli, R. (Eds.). *Changing Identities in Higher Education. Voicing Perspectives.* (pp.40-54). London & New York: Routledge

Land, R., Meyer, J.H.F., & Smith, J. (Eds.) (2008). *Threshold Concepts within the Disciplines.* Rotterdam: Sense Publishers

Leder, G.C. (1995). Higher degree research supervision: a question of balance. In *The Australian Universities' Review.* Vol.38, No.2, pp.5-8

Leonard, D. (2001). *A Women's Guide to Doctoral Studies*. Maidenhead: Open University Press

Lee, A. (2012). *Successful Research Supervision. Advising Students Doing Research.* London & New York: Routledge

Lee, A. (2008). How are doctoral students supervised? Concepts of research supervision. *Studies in Higher Education.* 33.4: 267-281

Lee, A. & Danby, S. (Eds.) (2012). *Reshaping Doctoral Education. International approaches and pedagogies.* London & New York: Routledge

Lévinas, E. (2003). *Totality and Infinity. An Essay on Exteriority.* Translated by Alphonso Lingis. Pittsburgh, Pennsylvania: Duquesne University Press

Lévinas, E. (2000). *Otherwise than Being or Beyond Essence.* Translated by Alphonso Lingis. Pittsburgh, Pennsylvania: Duquesne University Press

Levitt, D.H. (2001). Active Listening and Counselor Self-Efficacy: Emphasis on One Microskill in Beginning Counselor Training. *The Clinical Supervisor.* Vol. 20, No. 2, pp.101-115

Lien, T. (2011). *Veiledningens Hemmelighet. Læring og relasjoner.* Bergen: Fagbokforlaget

Lingis, A. (2007). *The First Person Singular.* Evanston, Illinois: Northwestern University Press

Lingis, A. (1998). *The Imperative.* Bloomington & Indianapolis: Indiana University Press

Lingis, A. (1996). *Sensation: Intelligibility in Sensibility.* New York: Humanity Books

Mainhard, T., van der Rijst, R., van Tartwijk, J. & Wubbels, T. (2009). A model for the supervisor-doctoral student relationship. *Higher Education*, 58, 359-373 DOI: 10.1007/s10734-009-9199-8

Malfroy, J. (2005). Doctoral supervision, workplace research and changing pedagogic practices. *Higher Education Research and Development.* Vol.24, No.2, pp.165-178

Manathunga, C. (2014). *Intercultural Postgraduate Supervision: Reimagining time, place and knowledge.* London & New York: Routledge

Manathunga, C. (2009). Post-colonial perspectives on interdisciplinary researcher identities. In Brew, A. & Lucas, L. (Eds.). *Academic Research and Researchers.* Berkshire: Open University Press

Manathunga, C. (2007). Supervision as mentoring: the role of power and boundary crossing. *Studies in Continuing Education.* Vol. 29, No. 2, pp.207-221

Manathunga, C. (2005). The Development of Research Supervision: "Turning the light on a private space". *International Journal for Academic Development.* Vol.10, No.1, pp.17-30

Manathunga, C. (2005b). Early warning signs in postgraduate research education: a different approach to ensuring timely completions. *Teaching in Higher Education.* Vol. 10, No. 2, pp.219-233

Manathunga, C. & Goozée, J. (2007). Challenging the dual assumption of the 'always/already' autonomous student and effective supervisor. *Teaching in Higher Education.* Vol. 12, No. 3, pp.309-322

Manen, M.v. & Adams, C. (2009). The phenomenology of space in writing online. In Dall'Alba, G. (Ed.). *Exploring education through phenomenology: Diverse approaches.* Oxford: Wiley-Blackwell

Marcel, G. (1952). *Metaphysical Journal.* Translated by Bernard Wall. Chicago: Henry Regnery Company

Määttä, K. (2012). *Obsessed with the Doctoral Theses. Supervision and Support during the Dissertation Process.* Rotterdam: Sense Publishers

McAlpine, L. & Amundsen, C. (Eds.) (2011). *Doctoral Education: Researched-Based Strategies for Doctoral Students, Supervisors and Administrators.* Springer Publishing

McAlpine, L. & McKinnon, M. (2013). Supervision – the most variable of variables: student perspectives. *Studies in Continuing Education*, Vol.35, No.3, pp.265-280

McAlpine, L. & Norton, J. (2006). Reframing our approach to doctoral programs: A learning perspective. *Higher Education Research and Development*, 25(1), 3-17

McAlpine, L. & Åkerlind, G. (2010). *Becoming an Academic. International Perspectives.* New York: Palgrave Macmillan

McDaniels, M. (2010). Doctoral Student Socialization for Teaching Roles. In Gardner, S.K. & Mendoza, P. (Eds.). *On Becoming a Scholar. Socialization and Development in Doctoral Education.* Sterling, Virginia: Stylus Publishing

McMichael, J. & McKee, M. (2008). Research Supervision: An Important Site of Teaching. *Journal of Teaching in Social Work.* Vol.28:1-2, pp.53-70

McPherson, I. (2011). Other than the Other. Levinas and the Educational Questioning of Infinity. In Egéa-Kuehne, D. (Ed.). *Levinas and Education. At the Intersection of Faith and Reason.* New York & London: Routledge

Mitchell, J. & Louw, W. (2011). Learning to Dance and Dancing to learn. In Nygaard, C., Courtney, N., & Frick, L. *Postgraduate Education – Form and Function.* Faringdon: Libri Publishing

Morley, L., Leonard, D. & David, M. (2002). Variations in Vivas: Quality and equality in British PhD assessment. *Studies in Higher Education.* Vol.27, No.3, pp.263-273

Mullen, C.A. & Tuten, E.M. (2010). Doctoral Cohort Mentoring. Interdependence, Collaborative Learning, and Cultural Change. *Scholar-Practitioner Quarterly.* Vol.4, No.1, pp.11-32

Murray, R. (2011). *How to Write a Thesis.* Berkshire: Open University Press

Murray, R. (2009). *How to Survive Your Viva: Defending a Thesis in an Oral Examination.* Berkshire: Open University Press

Nygaard, C., Courtney, N., & Frick, L. (2011). *Postgraduate Education – Form and Function.* Faringdon: Libri Publishing

Oinas, O. (2012). In Wonderland – How to supervise a Fox?. In Määttä, K. (Ed.). *Obsessed with the Doctoral Theses. Supervision and Support during the Dissertation Process.* Rotterdam: Sense Publishers

Parker, J. (2005). A Mise-en-Scène for the Theatrical University. In Barnett, R.

(red.). *Reshaping the University. New Relations between Research, Scholarship and Teaching.* Berkshire: Open University Press

Pearce, L. (2004). *How to Examine a Thesis.* Berhshire: Open University Press

Pearson, M. & Brew, A. (2002). Research Training and Supervision Development. *Studies in Higher Education,* Vol.27, No.2, pp.135-150

Pearson, M. & Kayrooz, C. (2004). Enabling critical reflection on research supervisory practice. *International Journal for Academic Development.* Vol. 9, No. 1, pp.99-116

Peelo, M. (2011). *Understanding Supervision and the PhD.* London & New York: Continuum

Petre, M. & Rugg, G. (2010). *The Unwritten Rules of PhD Research.* Berkshire: McGraw Hill, The Open University Press

Petre, M. & Rugg, G. (2011). *The Unwritten Rules of PhD Research.* Berkshire: Open University Press

Phillips, E.M. & Pugh, D.S. (2012). *How To Get a PhD. A handbook for students and their supervisors.* Berkshire: Open University Press

Price, D.C. & Money, A.H. (2002). Alternative Models for Doctoral Mentor Organisation and Research Supervision. *Mentoring & Tutoring.* Vol. 10, No. 2, pp.127-135

Rogers, C. (2004). *On Becoming a Person. A therapist's view of psychotherapy.* London: Constable

Rogers, C. (2003). *Client-Centered Therapy.* London: Constable

Rowley, D.J. & Sherman, H. (2004). *Supervision in Colleges and Universities.* Lanham: University Press of America

Rudd, E. (1985). *A New Look at Postgraduate Failure.* Guildford, Surrey: The Society for Research into Higher Education

Rudd, E. (1975). *The Highest Education. A Study of Graduate Education in Britain.* London & Boston: Routledge & Kegan Paul

Rudd, E. (1968). *Graduate study and after.* London: Weidenfeld & Nicolson

Selwyn, N. (2014). *Digital Technology and the Contemporary University. Degrees of Digitalization.* London & New York: Routledge

Selwyn, N. (2013). *Distrusting Educational Technology. Critical Questions for Changing Times.* London & New York: Routledge

Shields, C.M. & Edwards, M.M. (2005). *Dialogue is Not Just Talk. A New Ground for Educational Leadership.* New York: Peter Lang

Shipley, S.D. (2010). Listening: A Concept Analysis. *Nursing Forum.* Vol. 45, No. 2, pp.125-134

Starke-Meyerring, D. (2011). The Paradox of Writing in Doctoral Education: Student Experiences. IN McAlpine & Amundsen (Eds.). *Doctoral Education: Researched-Based Strategies for Doctoral Students, Supervisors and Administrators.* Springer Publishing

Sternberg, R. J. (2010). *Thinking Styles.* Cambridge University Press

Sussex, R. (2008). Technological options in supervising remote research students. *Higher Education.* Vol. 55, pp. 121-137

Taylor, S. & Beasley, N. (2010). *A Handbook for Doctoral Supervisors*. London & New York: Routledge

Tinkler, P. & Jackson, C. (2004). *The Doctoral Examination Process: A Handbook for Students, Examiners and Supervisors*. Berkshire: Open University Press

Trafford, V. & Leshem, S. (2012). *Stepping Stones to Achieving your Doctorate: Focusing on your viva from the start*. Berkshire: Open University Press

Tulloch, L. (2013). Fantasy, resistance and passion as important aspects of the doctoral writing process. In Engels-Schwarzpaul, A.-Chr. & Peters, M.A. *Of Other Thoughts: Non-Traditional Ways to the Doctorate. A Guidebook for Candidates and Supervisors*. Rotterdam: Sense Publishers

Turner, G. (2015). Learning to supervise: four journeys. Learning to supervise: four journeys. *Innovations in Education and Teaching International*, 52:1, 86-98, DOI: 10.1080/14703297.2014.981840

Turunen, T. (2012). From the Countdown to an Intermediate Stopping Point. In Määttä, K. *Obsessed with the Doctoral Theses. Supervision and Support during the Dissertation Process*. Rotterdam: Sense Publishers

Walker, G.E., Golde, C.M., Jones, L., Bueschel, A.C., & Hutchings, P. (2008). *The Formation of Scholars. Rethinking Doctoral Education for the Twenty-First Century*. San Francisco: Jossey-Bass

Weidman, J.C. (2010). Doctoral Student Socialization for Research. In Gardner, S.K. & Mendoza, P. (Eds.). *On Becoming a Scholar. Socialization and Development in Doctoral Education*. Sterling, Virginia: Stylus Publishing

Welsh, J. (1982). Improving the supervision of postgraduate students. *Research in Education*. May issue, 0, 27, pp.1-8

Welsh, J. (1981). The PhD Student at Work. *Studies in Higher Education*. Vol.6, No.2, pp.159-162

Welsh, J. (1978). The supervision of postgraduate research students. *Research in Education*. Vol. 19, pp.77-86

Whitely, A. (2012). Supervisory conversations on rigour and interpretive research. *Qualitative Research Journal*. Vol. 12, No. 2, pp.251-271

Willetts, J., Mitchell, C., Abeysuriya, K., & Fam, D. (2012). Creative tensions. Negotiating the multiple dimensions of a transdisciplinary doctorate. In Lee, A. & Danby, S. (Eds.). *Reshaping Doctoral Education. International approaches and pedagogies*. London & New York: Routledge

Wisker, G. (2012). *The Good Supervisor*. New York: Palgrave Macmillan

Wisker, G. (2008). *The Postgraduate Research Handbook*. New York: Palgrave Macmillan

Wisker, G. & Robinson, G. (2012). Picking up the pieces: supervisors and doctoral "orphans". *International Journal for Researcher Development*. Vol.3, No.2, pp.139-153

Wisker, G. & Robinson, G. (2009). Encouraging postgraduate students of literature and art to cross conceptual thresholds. *Innovations in Education and Teaching International*. Vol.46, No.3, August 2009, pp.317-330

Wisker, G., Robinson, G., Trafford, V., Warnes, M., & Creighton, E. (2003). From Supervisory Dialogues to Successful PhDs: strategies supporting and enabling the learning conversations of staff and students at postgraduate level. *Teaching in Higher Education*. Vol.8, No.3, pp.383-397

Zukas, M. & Andersen, L.L. (2012). Taking a break. Doctoral Summer School as transformative pedagogies. IN Lee, A. & Danby, S. (Eds.) *Reshaping Doctoral Education. International approaches and pedagogies.* London & New York: Routledge